The New York Times

VERY PUNNY PUZZLES

The New York Times

VERY PUNNY PUZZLES
75 Clever Crosswords from the Pages of
The New York Times

Edited by Will Shortz

ST. MARTIN'S GRIFFIN ❧ NEW YORK

ACROSS

1 It's in a jamb
5 Schoolmarmish
9 Outback Bowl city
14 To boot
15 NBC host
16 N.B.A. star called "The Shack"
17 Stout ingredient
18 Regarding
19 Hardly cutting-edge
20 Computer business?
22 Bit of color
23 Guitarist Paul
24 Sipping specialist
25 Rifle attachment
29 Show place
32 NATO members
34 Nature of cyberspace?
39 Wash out
40 Center
42 Suffix with buck
43 Combining on the Internet?
45 Risk
47 Synthetic fiber
49 Tetra- plus one
50 Say
54 Bolivian bear
56 Chili rating unit?
57 What makes people write LOL?
63 Christina Applegate sitcom
64 Litter's littlest
65 Name that rings a bell?
66 Writer Chekhov
67 Manger visitors
68 Sitar music
69 Doesn't possess
70 Gulf of ___, off the coast of Yemen
71 Feel sure about

DOWN

1 Woman of rank
2 Haakon's royal successor
3 2-Down's capital
4 Univ. marchers
5 Part of a service
6 Put up a fight
7 Division word
8 Phobos, to Mars
9 Mexicali munchie
10 Opposition
11 Had in mind
12 Satchel in Cooperstown
13 Birch relative
21 Sheltered, at sea
24 Kind of serum
25 Cracker's target
26 Symbol of happiness
27 Ye follower
28 Place for a shore dinner
30 Alternative to a fence
31 Binet data
33 Brat's look
35 Take it easy
36 Qum home
37 Reason for a suit
38 Skywalker's mentor
41 Roadside stop
44 Piece of clothing
46 Each
48 Lizard's locale?
50 Indian chief
51 "Maria ___" (old tune)
52 Brig's pair
53 Gasoline may make it go
55 Protest of a sort
57 Witty Bombeck
58 Campus area
59 Picnic spot
60 Russian Everyman
61 Canceled, to NASA
62 Nibble away

by Richard Silvestri

2

ACROSS

1 Hardly a close contest
5 Marching band section
10 À la mode
14 Biblical preposition
15 Still
16 It may be minced
17 The latest
18 "The Prince of Tides" star
19 ___ Minor
20 Aim
22 Underwater worker
24 Picket sign for a Cape Canaveral technician?
27 "Peer Gynt" character
28 Prudential competitor
32 Madame Bovary
36 Frightening word
37 Golden ___
38 Get fatter faster?
41 Foul (up)
42 Major club
43 Nudge
44 Candied
45 Levelheaded
47 Farm animal's anatomical pronouncement?
53 Colorful playing marble
56 Reduced
57 Baseball manager Felipe
58 Yale of Yale University
61 Gung-ho
62 Use a spoon, in a way
63 Country album?
64 Clique
65 Mender's target
66 Airbase near Lubbock
67 Sommer in the movies

DOWN

1 Dustup
2 Bridge bid, briefly
3 Calendar run
4 Toughie
5 Explosive situation
6 Certain numero
7 ___ canto
8 Calculating
9 Back
10 Paid reluctantly
11 Disservice
12 Lead-in to shame or boy
13 "The Chinese Parrot" hero
21 Cook's hair wear
23 City due west of Daytona Beach
25 Spoils
26 Song whose title translates as "Farwell to Thee"

29 First baseman Martinez
30 Where to go for the jugular
31 King Arthur of the courts
32 Goes back to sea?
33 Catty remark
34 Like a parent who can't bear you?
35 Idle
37 Welcoming party
39 Obligation at some churches
40 Its cap. is Quito
45 Slim and trim
46 One of the 12 tribes of Israel
48 Per annum
49 Utility bill basis
50 Like some ships at sea
51 Sound at a toast

52 Equivocate
53 Long green
54 Kind of sax
55 Hard work
59 ___ de la Réunion
60 Is down with

by Manny Nosowsky

3

ACROSS

1 Trifle
7 Scenery spoiler
11 "Kapow!"
14 Pleistocene Epoch, familiarly
15 Come into view
16 Skilled horseman of the Old West
17 Roads to wedded bliss?
19 Sign of success
20 Any old town
21 Grand party
22 End of 14-Across
23 Timeline sections
25 Beach accessory
28 Prenuptial nerves?
32 See 63-Across
33 Nix from Nixon, e.g.
34 Bossy boss
36 Artist Rousseau
38 Give it ___
40 Stake
41 Director's cry
43 Ancient Andean
45 Altdorf's canton
46 Snort of a confirmed bachelor?
49 Quality camera
50 Word processing command
51 It may be critical
53 Campus marchers: Abbr.
55 The last Mrs. Chaplin
59 Latin trio leader
60 Advice to a wannabe princess?
63 With 32-Across, a 1983 Lionel Richie hit
64 Horace tome
65 "Wait Till the Sun Shines" girl
66 Nile reptile
67 Stag, in a way
68 Renders unyielding

DOWN

1 The "Gee" in Bee Gees
2 Hose hue
3 Small dam
4 Potato peeler, e.g.
5 Turkish honorific
6 Prosperity
7 Part of a farm feeder
8 Some church music
9 "That feels good!"
10 A.L. or N.L. V.I.P.'s
11 Amateurish
12 Razor brand
13 Siamese-speak
18 100 centimos
22 Prefix with -zene
24 It has full pockets
26 Baseball's Master Melvin
27 Disobedient
28 Betel palm
29 Vegetarian protein source
30 Stray from the herd
31 Quite a dummy
32 "That's it!"
35 Prefix with athlete
37 Gets promoted
39 Taxi sign
42 Japanese computer giant
44 Things people do to get their kicks?
47 Speed (along)
48 Noggin
51 Poet Angelou
52 Pop singer Tori
54 About
56 Heraldic border
57 Diamond of music
58 Bowls over
60 Calendar pages: Abbr.
61 Big deal
62 Bottom line

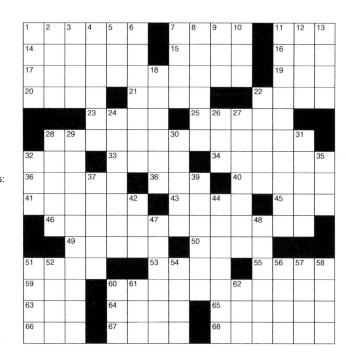

by Nancy Salomon and Sherry O. Blackard

4

ACROSS

1 Vaulted space
5 Go door to door, perhaps
10 Quisling's city
14 Spring, maybe
15 Freezer brand
16 Conversant with
17 Jury members meditate?
19 Salts
20 ___ fraîche
21 Try for a part
22 Cremona cabbage
23 Gutter neighbor
25 Presidential appointees
27 Ask, as for aid
30 Phil Esposito and teammates
31 Touch on
32 Edible root
34 Place for a pickup
37 The Eagle that landed
38 In starts in seven days
40 Foreman's superior
41 "Time in a Bottle" singer
43 Love ___
44 Bearing
45 Gone bad
47 Mean
49 On the block
51 Nordstrom rival
52 "No way!"
53 Start of a break-in
55 Start of a Christmas song
59 Judi Dench, for one
60 Posed among fancy sheets?
62 Snowball
63 Ruler of Hades
64 Storage cylinder
65 Pencil holders, sometimes
66 More knavish
67 Clucking sounds

DOWN

1 Current choice
2 Robin's beneficiaries
3 8 1/2, e.g.
4 Nickel, but not dime
5 Heel
6 Love, Italian-style
7 Level
8 Apse location, today
9 Four-wheeled carriage
10 Silhouette, essentially
11 Resort on the Costa del Sol?
12 "M" star
13 Get-go
18 Straight up
24 Stand up and be counted
26 Presidential runs
27 One end of the Mohs' scale
28 Over in Berlin
29 Gossipy bartender's choices?
30 Produce in a reactor
33 Best Picture of 1977
35 He had designs on Jackie
36 Like champagne bubbles
38 Actress Rowlands
39 "___ deal!"
42 They're nuts
44 Like Don Knotts as Rambo
46 They may help obtain closure
48 Bout enders, in brief
49 Falsify, in a way
50 Name on Tara's deed
51 Clobber, biblically
54 Pincushion alternative
56 Miss ___ of song
57 Draw out
58 Grandson of Adam
61 Swe. neighbor

by Greg Staples

ACROSS

1 Luciano Pavarotti, e.g.
6 Bomb
10 Lip-balm target
14 Addis ___
15 Gift for a diva
16 Moneyed one
17 Candlestick maker?
19 Ever's partner
20 Like some inspections
21 Mukluk material
23 Nintendo rival
25 Tankard filler
26 Laudatory lines
27 Seductresses
31 Narcissist's love
33 He floated "like a butterfly"
34 Sports buff's memorization
36 Post-op time
39 Mugger subduer
41 Give an address
43 It's a long story
44 Spot often struck by a snake
46 Snake, to Medusa
48 "Am ___ a roll!"
49 Portraitists' purchases
51 Power up, as an old battery
53 Pound sound
55 Schlep
57 Sound of a tuned engine
58 Within reach, as a solution
61 State of confusion
65 Annual theater award
66 Chef?
68 Winter coating
69 Warhol pal ___ Sedgwick
70 Oral Roberts University site
71 Yemeni port
72 Student overseer
73 Hypnotist's word

DOWN

1 South Seas food staple
2 Israel's Abba
3 Some floor votes
4 Double-reed player
5 Some river travelers
6 Busy night at a bar: Abbr.
7 Old cabin materials
8 Milo of "The Verdict"
9 Parts of bloomers
10 Cartoonist Addams, for short
11 Barber?
12 Steer clear of
13 Rigatoni relative
18 Smooth, musically
22 Groucho-type look
24 In pieces
27 Doll's cry
28 Conservative Keyes
29 Watchmaker?
30 Brenda of the comics
32 "___ Misérables"
35 Pricey
37 Bug-eyed
38 Ruination
40 "Boola Boola" collegian
42 Portuguese monetary unit
45 Actress Raines
47 Old-time impositions of penance
50 Came off the bench (for)
52 Like a literary Dodger
53 Prefix with phobia
54 Make another offer
56 Fly smoothly
59 Archie or Jughead
60 Director Kazan
62 In fine fettle
63 Irish Gaelic
64 Swing a scythe
67 Gridiron great Dawson

by Fred Piscop

6

ACROSS

1 What this puzzle is designed to elicit
4 N.H.L. Northeast Division player
9 Chap
14 Fun, for short
15 "That is to say . . ."
16 Like a nerd
17 Bubble maker
18 "Enough rain already!"?
20 Tax chart divisions
22 Addles
23 Certain frosh
24 Noodle
25 Dress for the desert?
28 Infantile outburst
31 Get rid of wrinkles
32 Not be brave
33 "Primal Fear" star
34 Operetta princess and others
35 Southern dish
37 Turnarounds, informally
38 Clone
39 Aragón article
40 Astrological chart divisions
41 Hosp. areas
42 Mountain resort famous for its breath mints?
45 Kind of rock
46 Free-spoken
47 As part of a company
50 "The Seduction of Joe Tynan" star
53 Departed a sheikdom?
55 Natalie Cole hit "___ Love"
56 Certain corn chip
57 Italy's ___ di Pisa
58 Salon job
59 Side in a debate

60 Visual putdown
61 Pig ___

DOWN

1 Sheik, e.g.
2 Child of fortune?
3 Places for spare parts, maybe
4 Some pitches
5 It multiplies by dividing
6 Licked
7 Chorus from the sidelines
8 Abbr. in a business letter
9 Con's misfortune
10 Frighten
11 At the home of
12 Biblical herd
13 Selects, with "for"
19 A whole lot
21 Stylish

24 Very dry, as wine
25 Enliven, with "up"
26 Hot blood
27 Hand-holder?
28 Fast result?
29 "There ___ free lunches"
30 "Steppenwolf" author
33 Vast tropical region of South America
35 Baum's good witch
36 Firm foundation
40 Major upset
42 Engines with oomph
43 With tantaras galore
44 Eau ___, Wis.
45 Page of music
47 Romeo introducer?
48 Home of the Universal Postal Union

49 "Just for the heck ___ . . ."
50 Elvis's middle name
51 Two-piece?
52 Too-too
54 Elevs.

by Manny Nosowsky

ACROSS

1 "___," said Tom presently
5 Not chronic
10 Limey's quaff
14 N.Y.S.E. competitor
15 General denial?
16 Big partygoer?
17 "___," said Tom unremittingly
20 Hood's gun
21 Pond cover
22 Gladiator's place
23 On the main
24 Word before juris or generis
25 "___," said Tom fittingly
33 Snappish
34 Meadow denizen
35 Symbol of solidity
36 Suggestive
37 It was tested on Bikini, 1954
39 Polynesian amulet figure
40 "Little" Stowe girl
41 "Fudge!"
42 Baffler
43 "___," said Tom accordingly
47 Bettor's interest
48 Differently
49 Pretend
52 Utterly destroyed
54 State touching Can.
57 "___," said Tom patiently
60 All you can eat
61 Early settlers of Iceland
62 Top
63 Provokes splenetically
64 Emulates Babe Ruth
65 "___," said Tom haltingly

DOWN

1 Reagan cabinet member
2 Mme. Bovary
3 Let
4 Outside: Prefix
5 "Crouching Tiger, Hidden Dragon" director
6 Jackie who starred in "Tom Sawyer," 1930
7 Voice of America org.
8 It has a point
9 Work unit
10 "All in the Family" role
11 Ready for plucking
12 Saudi Arabia neighbor
13 Maja painter
18 Nice to nosh
19 Gray-brown
23 Aesthetically pretentious
24 Macedonian's neighbor
25 Spread around
26 Cry to anchor men
27 "Platoon" prize
28 Sandal strap
29 Many a skit actor
30 Complaints
31 Bilked
32 Evade
37 Dangle
38 Lifting device
39 Webster's Unabridged, e.g.
41 Sawyer of ABC
42 Linguine sauce
44 "Communist Manifesto" co-author
45 Feed
46 Gets around
49 Poodle name
50 Mideast ruler
51 Man, but not Woman
52 Be sure
53 Uttar Pradesh tourist site
54 Hankering
55 Spanish building topper
56 Quarter
58 Politicos with jobs
59 Raven's call

by Mel Taub and crossword class

8

ACROSS
1 Cremona craftsman
6 Exec, slangily
10 Groucho remark
14 Where dos are done
15 "Say it ain't so!"
16 High-rise locales
17 Plot of land
18 Newsprint need
19 Midmonth day
20 Famous last words
23 Classic tattoo
24 Have an effect (on)
25 Big do
28 No visible means of support?
31 Like pine scent
35 Thai relative
36 Features of some locks
38 Bring together
39 Famous last words
42 Folded food items
43 Temple text
44 62-Across holiday
45 Back talk, slangily
47 Baseball mitt part
48 Nozzle site
49 "Zip-__-Doo-Dah"
51 Queenside castle, in chess notation
53 Famous last words
60 C-worthy?
61 Good student's reward
62 Capital on the Red River
63 Mountain road sign abbr.
64 Aloha State bird
65 Everglades bird
66 Used to be
67 Song and dance, e.g.
68 Film units

DOWN
1 Spot of wine?
2 Sting target
3 Astronaut Bean
4 In the offing
5 Divided
6 Soaks (up)
7 "Nah!"
8 How a trucker might go up a hill
9 Worst seats in the house
10 Short snort
11 Indic language
12 Skeptic's scoff
13 Ltr. addenda
21 Boundary
22 Slop holder
25 Travels like Tinker Bell
26 Patronize, as a restaurant
27 "Vissi d'arte" opera
29 Spellbound
30 O.K.
32 Inflicted upon
33 Stock holders?
34 "Fiddler" matchmaker
36 Square dance call
37 "Without a doubt!"
40 Capable of stooping to
41 Libreville's land
46 Plane name
48 Tribute
50 Fruity-smelling compound
52 Catchall column
53 Suburban pest
54 North Sea feeder
55 Have a yen for
56 Rock groups?
57 Legalistic phrase
58 Seasonal tune
59 E's, I's and S's, in Morse code
60 Needle

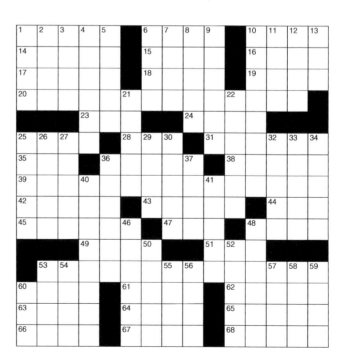

by Jay Sullivan

ACROSS

1 It can be poisonous
6 Flight fleet
10 One with idyll musings?
14 "Cosmicomics" author Calvino
15 A few words in passing?
16 1952 Olympics venue
17 Whence Sir Walter Scott's Fair Maid
18 Zola novel
19 Warbler
20 Stoppard play that made money abroad?
23 Letters for Old MacDonald
24 Mimosa-family tree
25 Cukor film that made money abroad?
29 Encouragement for Escamillo
30 Three-time Masters champ
31 Part of I.R.T.
35 Biblical verb
37 Indian attire
39 Central point
40 On a 42-Across
42 Knockabout, e.g.
44 Just out
45 Rolling Stones hit that made money abroad?
48 Acid neutralizer
51 Written commentary
52 Comedienne who made money abroad?
56 Give obligingly
57 Den din
58 Much-misunderstood writing
61 S-shaped molding

62 Tilted position
63 Follow
64 Microsoft product
65 Countercurrent
66 Swedish imports

DOWN

1 Very small serving
2 Indian tongue
3 Strict sergeants, say
4 Tennis great Gibson
5 Fortune sharers, perhaps
6 Mitchell with a guitar
7 Where bidders wait online
8 "Waterworld" actress Majorino
9 P.O.W.'s place
10 Indian confederacy founder
11 Courtier in "Hamlet"

12 Nicholas Gage novel
13 Friendly Islands
21 Some horses
22 N.E.A. member: Abbr.
23 Gulf of Aqaba port
25 Qatar's capital
26 Pick on
27 Country rocker Steve
28 No exemplar of erudition
32 Spread on Lake Tahoe
33 Head sets?
34 Moist
36 Announced
38 Boating locale
41 Annual song title starter
43 State symbols of Indiana

46 Run through
47 Clavicle connectors
48 Visibly happy
49 "Hasta ___!"
50 Seven-time N.L. home run champ
53 It may be hogged
54 "We the Living" author
55 So-o-o-o SoHo
59 Gist
60 Survey choice

by Alan Arbesfeld

ACROSS

1 Calculate astrologically
5 Smart player
10 Stupefy
14 Recorded proceedings
15 Easily broken
16 Rubber-stamp
17 May dance, maybe
18 Pro follower
19 ___ Horn
20 Desk item that's nothing to sneeze at?
23 Japanese honorific
24 Bartlett relatives
28 Hollow
32 Eccentric
35 Originated
36 Ballet movement
37 Stat that's good when under 3.00
38 Folk group that's nothing to sneeze at?
42 Wee hour
43 Netman Nastase
44 Chilling
45 Vinegar flavoring
48 Tricky problem
49 Krupp works city
50 Deserving a spanking
51 70's–80's show that's nothing to sneeze at?
59 Corner after "GO"
62 1976 best seller that starts in Gambia
63 Lust after, visually
64 Differential attachment
65 Slacken
66 Job opening
67 Join of arc?
68 Work with clay
69 Big buildup

DOWN

1 Comics fellow who hangs out in a pub
2 Piece of property
3 Sign on the corner
4 Pack down
5 Brawl
6 Soak
7 Alpine river
8 "La Bohème" heroine
9 Smeltery refuse
10 Person who's been given the third degree?
11 Blotter letters
12 Microwave
13 Real looker
21 Aromatic compound
22 TNT alternative
25 Sullies
26 1976 film featuring telekinesis
27 Buffy is one
28 "Breakfast at Tiffany's" author
29 Action centers
30 Electorate
31 Expert ending
32 Fagged
33 Nasty comments
34 Wedding page word
36 Ralph Lauren brand
39 Kind of iron
40 What alimony covers, minimally
41 ___ culpa
46 Staggered
47 Singer DiFranco
48 Dangler
50 Please, abroad
52 15.432 grains
53 Odd jobs doer
54 Loathsome one
55 Bag of chips, maybe
56 Unappealing
57 Lay an egg
58 It may be an honor
59 Shoot the breeze
60 Let go
61 Laid up

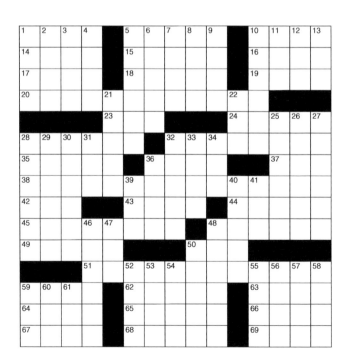

by Richard Silvestri

ACROSS

1 Staff figure
6 Hull hazard
10 Cast off
14 Steamed
15 Expression
16 Rhode Island's motto
17 Be affected by electrical attraction?
20 Time or life follower
21 It may be tipped
22 Next up
23 Israel's Netanyahu, familiarly
25 Profit share
26 Bishop preparing to hold a yard sale?
34 Young 'un
35 Architectural order
36 An inspiration to Beethoven
37 Server's edge, to Sampras
39 Broods
41 Sen. Bayh
42 Windows applications?
44 Track specialist
46 Work on a platter
47 Workout for bratty kids at a mountain resort?
50 Day-care diversion
51 F.B.I. figures
52 Draft
56 Shad ___
58 Part of a Latin trio
61 Apt title for this puzzle
64 Warts and all
65 No good deed
66 Dress with a flare
67 Positive reply
68 Turn down
69 Moisten

DOWN

1 Band's schedule
2 Field goal?
3 Like most citizens
4 Like some cuisine
5 Charge
6 Pet peeve?
7 Football great Ronnie
8 Swooning sound
9 Barely make
10 Like many horses
11 Perfect
12 Big production
13 Education station
18 They're thick-skinned
19 With 55-Down, where some things come out
24 Two hearts, e.g.
25 Coop cry
26 "The Bell Jar" writer
27 Arm bones
28 Cross
29 Paramecia features
30 Word of encouragement
31 Help that's always available
32 Father of famous twins
33 Some change
38 Greatest possible
40 "The Battleship Potemkin" director Eisenstein
43 Get out of a slump?
45 It stores data permanently
48 Disposed of, with "up"
49 Snoopy, e.g.
52 Time of reckoning
53 Hillock
54 What one of the five Olympic rings stands for
55 See 19-Down
56 Picnicker's worry
57 It's near Paris
59 Rough problem to face?
60 Brood
62 Member of the first family
63 Collar

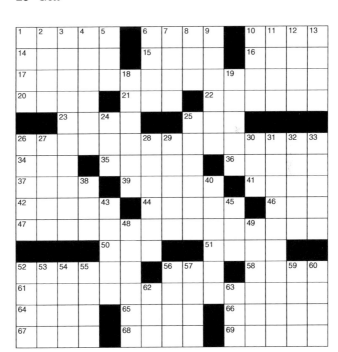

by Joe DiPietro

ACROSS

1 1976 Best Picture
6 Discontinue
10 Tuna __
14 Foolish
15 Thumbs-up write-up
16 Copycat
17 Affect strangely
18 "A Death in the Family" writer
19 Go all over
20 See 38-Across
23 Friend of Fidel
25 Voluminous ref. set
26 Minces
27 Churchill called it "soul-destroying"
30 Adversary
31 "Our Father which __ heaven . . ."
32 Court entertainer
34 Plan of action
38 With 53-Across, a daffynition of 20-Across
41 Cicero's existence
42 Unsubstantial
43 Australian predator
44 Mess up
45 Military awards
46 Iroquois Confederacy tribe
50 Handle some hills
52 Get the picture
53 See 38-Across
57 Sported
58 Egg on
59 Flip response?
62 "What __?"
63 Plotting
64 Angler's accessory
65 Fizzles out
66 They're crossable
67 Rash

DOWN

1 Part of a cage
2 Formula __
3 Blockbuster rentals
4 Nautical unit
5 Mysterious Himalayan
6 Des Moines university
7 Fulminated
8 Done with
9 Resident's security device
10 His 1961 record had an asterisk
11 Historical period
12 River embankment
13 Lock of hair
21 New England catch
22 Charlotte of "The Facts of Life"
23 Overstarched collar problem
24 Long-eared animals
28 Good news on Wall Street
29 Business letter abbr.
30 Mossback
32 Place for a ride
33 Eight-time Norris Trophy winner
34 Footnote abbr.
35 Chou and others
36 Scout rank
37 Win by __
39 Scolding
40 1952 political inits.
44 Old French coin
45 Russian for peace
46 Did some carpentry
47 Meat problem
48 Sip
49 Fencing needs
50 Union member
51 Praise
54 Text
55 Result of a bite, maybe
56 Mystery writer Paretsky
60 Court ruling?
61 Surreptitious

by Sarah Keller

ACROSS

1 Labor Day and many other fed. holidays
5 Canterbury can
9 "Auld Lang ___"
13 Eastern nurse
14 Slow, on a score
15 Where homeys hang
16 Lamb's meat made of building blocks?
18 Got on in years
19 Six Flags New England locale
20 Utah state flower
22 For most movie audiences
24 ___ y Plata (Montana's motto)
25 Decision regarding a Belafonte song?
31 Picture holder
34 1989 Oscar winner Jessica
35 Susan of "The Partridge Family"
36 Guilty one, in copspeak
37 Lion tamers' needs
38 Wine label info
39 Sister of Zsa Zsa
40 Sound on the hour
41 Totaled, costwise
42 Place for assenting Brits?
45 Ltd., here
46 Foxhole occupant
50 Guaranteed to work
55 Sen. Feinstein
56 Airline since 1948
57 Beatle's maxim?
59 Add fringe to
60 Subordinate Clauses?
61 Oozy ground
62 Hammer or sickle
63 Roy Rogers's real surname
64 Rose part

DOWN

1 Of the cheek
2 Alpha's opposite
3 Bother persistently
4 Made the scene
5 Comprehend
6 Black or red insects
7 Platte River Indian
8 A million to one, say
9 Haifa hello
10 One who sits cross-legged, maybe
11 Christmas
12 Water awhirl
14 Like inferior gravy
17 Sir's mate
21 Unrestrained revelry
23 Like some romances
26 "I love," to Yvette
27 Sets free
28 Genesis garden
29 "Cool!"
30 Newbie
31 Mimic
32 First name in jeans
33 Toot one's own horn
37 "So?"
38 Sail supports
40 Boxes: Abbr.
41 Kindled anew
43 Campus Jewish organization
44 Fusses
47 Mukluks wearer
48 ___ nous
49 Shorten again, perhaps
50 Pedal pushers
51 Designer Gucci
52 Othello's ensign
53 Plug up
54 A deadly sin
58 "How about that!"

by Kelly Clark

14

ACROSS
1 Targets for snakes
6 Arena shouts
10 Sec
14 Dumpy digs
15 It may be outstanding
16 Chanteuse Adams
17 Capital of Guam, old-style
18 Finito
19 Finito
20 Either way, the letter carrier's work not appreciated
23 Pickled delicacy
24 Clavell's "___-Pan"
25 Rather's network
28 Prefix with sweet
31 Zero in acting
36 Zuñi's cousin
38 Protuberance
40 "M" star
41 Either way, Cupid recognized my pain
44 Nosy Parker
45 Time for eggnog
46 The gamut
47 Court battle?
49 Sine language?
51 Mexican Mrs.
52 Estuary
54 Aurora's counterpart
56 Either way, country star shunned hip-hop
65 Jerusalem's Mosque of ___
66 Hoopster Bryant
67 Like some accents
68 Act the expectant father
69 Hibernia
70 Warren of "Dillinger"
71 Charon's river
72 Take five
73 60's poster genre

DOWN
1 It may have a dimple
2 Stadium section
3 Caplet shape
4 Wish granter
5 Breaks one's back
6 Household spray target
7 Tax
8 Critic Roger
9 Place to fish
10 Skywalker, e.g.
11 Elvis, once
12 Dandy
13 Satellite transmission
21 "Maria ___" (hit of 1941)
22 Early strings
25 Highboy or lowboy
26 Shouldered
27 Three wood
29 Like a neat yard
30 Blockhead
32 Cub with a club
33 Brings (out)
34 Overthrow, e.g.
35 First name in daytime talk
37 "The Heat ___"
39 It may have a fat lip
42 Veep before Gerald
43 1979 sci-fi thriller
48 Tricky pitch
50 Baby talk
53 Really dig
55 Holster part
56 Daddy-o
57 Part of a Latin trio
58 Risqué
59 Natural history museum display
60 Nile bird
61 Mar, in a way
62 Pro ___
63 Maintain
64 Dennis, to Mr. Wilson

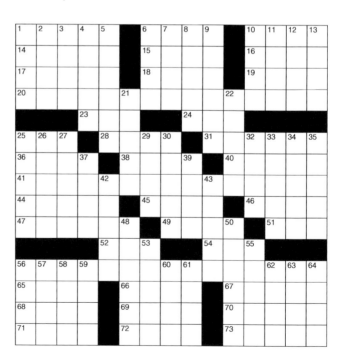

by Randall J. Hartman

ACROSS

1 Counterfeit
5 Innocent ones
10 Get steamed up
14 Landlocked ___ Sea
15 Hall of fame
16 Construction support
17 Wrongful act in Ankara?
19 Prosciutto purveyor
20 Letters of attorney?
21 Two-finger sign
22 Exclusive group
24 State of agitation
26 Surly sort
27 Longtime Susan Lucci role
29 Make pink?
33 Decoder feature
36 Loony
38 Looniness
39 Part of a plot
40 Garson of Hollywood
42 Cauterize
43 Wherewithal
45 Leaves home?
46 Sea swallow
47 J.F.K.'s 109
49 Sister of Clio
51 Johnstown disaster
53 Chihuahua wrap
57 Rarely seen haircut nowadays
60 Syndicate head
61 Neptune or Jupiter
62 Corporate image
63 Dud villages?
66 Old apple spray
67 Clear the slate
68 Le Pew of cartoons
69 On one's guard
70 Library device
71 Shade of blue

DOWN

1 "___ Attraction"
2 Oranjestad's island
3 Gold standard
4 Kiwanian colleague
5 Dress option for cold weather
6 Start the pot
7 Telephonic 6
8 Canoe material
9 Begin a journey
10 Oily Cuban?
11 Over in Germany
12 Algeria neighbor
13 War of 1812 battle site
18 At any time
23 Well-kept
25 Conservative beauty?
26 Handled a reception
28 Brusque
30 Prayer joint?
31 Comeback to an accusation
32 Pull down
33 Drizzly
34 "Body Count" rapper
35 Burnoose wearer
37 Tea leaf reader
41 Logician
44 Skeptic's grain
48 Drove (around)
50 Keep an eye on
52 "Norma," for one
54 See eye to eye
55 "Where's ___?" (George Segal movie)
56 Collectible car
57 Blemish
58 Name spelled out in a 1970 hit
59 Seaweed substance
60 Teaspoon or tablet, say
64 Automobile accessory
65 Be decisive

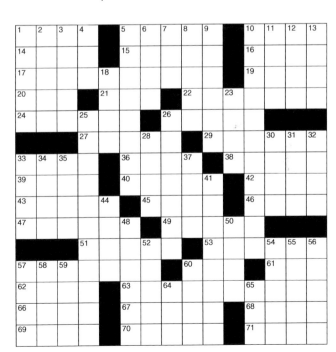

by Richard Silvestri

ACROSS

1 Magic practicer
7 What "Bethesda" means
13 Shout of praise
15 Goblet
16 With 37- and 38-Across, a musing
18 Lap dogs
19 Eastern "way"
20 Community spirit
21 "Brian's Song" or "Roots"
24 Big inits. in bowling
27 Historian Durant
28 ___-Bo exercise
31 Person with a stick
34 Beautyrest company
37 & 38 See 16-Across
39 They may get quarters downtown
41 Speech impediment?
42 Govt. medical agency
43 Kind of center
45 Sound after a puncture
46 1958 Edna Ferber novel
50 St. Teresa's town
53 Year in the Amazon
54 "___ the loneliest number"
58 16-, 37- and 38-Across, e.g.
61 Olympic Airways founder
62 Troublemaker
63 Tenant
64 Gauge

DOWN

1 U.P.S., say
2 British vice admiral in the American Revolution
3 "Dilbert" intern
4 Like a lion
5 "___ It Goes" (Ellerbee book)
6 San Antonio-to-Ft. Worth dir.
7 "Evita" role
8 Women's group
9 Prince Valiant's wife
10 Kind of helmet
11 Off-the-wall reply
12 Bottom of the barrel
14 Conductor Toscanini
15 Washing dishes, taking out the garbage, etc.
17 Dry wash
22 Actress Tia
23 "Arabian Nights" hero
24 Mideast capital
25 New Zealander
26 Dogs do it
28 Geometrical solid
29 "___ Ghost" (Michael Ondaatje novel)
30 Parts of car test courses
32 ___ Na Na
33 Film director Kotcheff
35 Computer unit, for short
36 Fold, spindle or mutilate
40 Poppy parts
41 Rubber
44 Mandlikova of tennis
46 "___ My Sugar in Salt Lake City" (1943 hit)
47 Grounds
48 Hooded covers
49 Organic compounds
50 Get an ___ effort
51 Turbine part
52 One-named supermodel
55 Iroquoian Indian
56 Union agreements?
57 I.R.S. ID's
59 Military address
60 Word with black or green

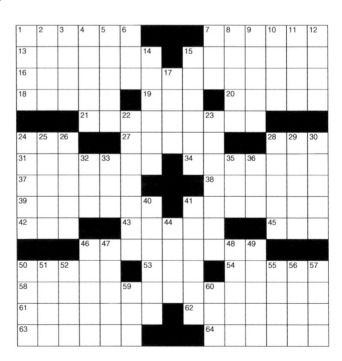

by Dave and Diane Epperson

ACROSS

1 Vets' concerns
5 Left so as to admit some light
9 It makes il mondo go round
14 Imperial, for example
15 Sultry
16 Expensive watch
17 Athlete's state?
19 Undemocratic law
20 Times in classifieds
21 Turner or Cole
22 It may follow well
23 Wee
25 Tiler's state?
27 Bit of gossip
28 In no time
29 Rebuffs overseas
30 It may be served on 8-Down
31 One of 18 rois
33 Test taker's state?
37 Animal with a snout
38 At first: Abbr.
40 Suffix with song
44 "With malice toward ___ . . .": Lincoln
45 Things peddled
47 Philosopher's state?
49 Carol starter
50 Singer Cara and others
51 A couple of cups?
52 ___ mater (brain cover)
53 1977 U.S. Open winner
54 Honeymooners' state?
57 Bad deeds
58 Hash
59 Numerical prefix
60 Toy named after a politician
61 Severe setback
62 Trivial Pursuit category: Abbr.

DOWN

1 Word after one or two
2 It's found in a table
3 Taut
4 IV, to III
5 Analysis
6 Not be serious
7 Pink-slip
8 Sandwich choice
9 "You ___ Casanova" (Mariah Carey lyric)
10 In step with fashion
11 Lover of Cesario, in "Twelfth Night"
12 Move away
13 They form a crowd in Hollywood
18 Certain coffee
22 Ancient region on the Aegean
24 Ted Williams wore it
25 "No ___!"
26 Paris attraction
28 Chemise, e.g.
32 Reason for kids to miss school
34 ___ Major
35 "Dies ___"
36 Pilot's zone
39 Enter
40 Nervous excitement
41 Flourish
42 Iris cover
43 1980's White House name
46 Experienced sailor
48 Having entanglements
49 Traffic marking
51 Vigor
54 Kind of scene
55 Everyone
56 Record keeper

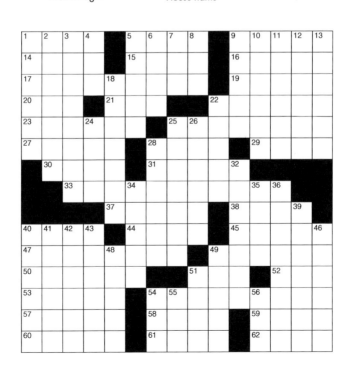

by Michael Shteyman

18

ACROSS

1 Brutish sort
6 Picture prize
11 Phone ___
14 Vice president Stevenson
15 Seize, à la Caesar
16 Masseur's supply
17 Insect's bedtime ritual?
19 Bother
20 Hole-in-one
21 King in a Steve Martin song
22 1945 conference site
24 Part of a service
26 Perfumes with a joss stick, say
27 Induction motor developer
29 Very funny person
32 Game show panelist Peggy
35 Preschoolers
37 "___ Mio"
38 "Bleah!"
39 Sass from Elsie?
41 Shell mover
42 Ragú rival
44 Milton Friedman's subj.
45 Friend of Big Bird
46 ___ Club
48 Dumbstruck
50 Hand down
52 Not stop for, in a way
56 Have in one's hands
58 Test site
59 Big D.C. lobby
60 Tick off
61 Sound when a gobbler gets a joke?
64 "Y" wearer
65 Actress Eleniak
66 Oscar-winning screenwriter Robert
67 Antonym's antonym: Abbr.
68 Knocks flat
69 Aligns

DOWN

1 Raisin cakes
2 Bring out
3 Ragged Dick creator
4 Carrier to Copenhagen
5 Move quietly
6 One ___ (ball game)
7 For example
8 Kind of sole
9 They have strings attached
10 Place to stretch your legs
11 Hammer for a hopper?
12 Disney musical
13 Latch (onto)
18 Totals
23 Tres y tres
25 Whitney and others: Abbr.
26 Puss's food container?
28 Game company that originated Yahtzee
30 Steamer, e.g.
31 Medal awardee, maybe
32 Putting targets
33 Prefix with cultural
34 Rams, lambs and ewes?
36 Move with difficulty
39 Dressed like a Victorian woman
40 Sort of
43 Fat, in France
45 Slippery sort
47 Make certain
49 Some beers
51 "Hamlet" courtier
53 Public, as information
54 Bucker
55 Director Peter
56 Bakers' wares
57 Alternative to De Gaulle
58 Pastoral places
62 Hateful org.
63 Today, in Toledo

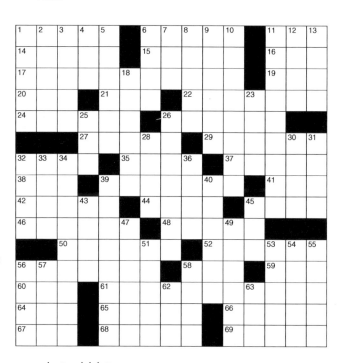

by Randolph Ross

ACROSS

1 "No ___!" (slangy reply)
5 They go back and forth to work
9 Suit
14 "The Labors of Hercules" painter Guido
15 Off ramp
16 Susan Lucci's Emmy role
17 "That's clear to me" in beat-speak
18 "___ Lisa"
19 "Santa Fe Songs" composer
20 Photo session at a farm?
23 Rental period
24 "You ___ bother . . ."
27 Place with a feed trough
28 Formally approve
33 Well-nigh
34 Full scale?
35 Overly sentimental
36 Remission of big toe inflammation?
38 Strongly hopes
40 Mountain airs
41 Tot's recitation
42 Latke ingredient
43 Hair knot
46 In this way
48 Call from a ward
50 Quantity for a European pastry chef?
55 Ordinary writing
57 Uncivil
58 Pest
59 Lake crosser
60 N.Y.S.E. relative
61 Falco of "The Sopranos"
62 Pass, as time
63 Difference of opinion
64 Convinced

DOWN

1 Light dispersers
2 Extremely popular
3 Like some salad dressings
4 One with a closed heart
5 Rest area sight
6 Bit of a nerve
7 Annex
8 Principal
9 1960's best-selling author Eric
10 Kind of zone
11 Grp. at a station
12 Cap material
13 Tufted topper
21 Violent struggles
22 In the least
25 Break of a sort
26 An encouraging word
29 Sandburg poem "___ Window"
30 City whose name means "eastern capital"
31 Dimwit
32 "The Grapes of Wrath" star, 1940
34 Tough time to farm
35 "Bye now"
36 Resolve
37 Pick up
38 Mate
39 Slugger's stat.
42 Gambler's desire
43 Godfather portrayer
44 Label on a street-corner box
45 Like Russian dolls
47 War horse
49 Recommends
51 Great times
52 Cut of beef
53 Proposal
54 Vaccinator's call
55 iMac competitors
56 Blame

by Manny Nosowsky

20

ACROSS
1 Political group
5 ___ it out
10 God of the Canaanites
14 Highlands hillside
15 Tamarack tree
16 Planting unit
17 Telegraph, say
18 Less cordial
19 Takes another direction
20 Baseball All-Star Game playing field?
23 Delphi figure
25 She loved Lancelot
26 "Enough!" in El Salvador
27 Player of "As Time Goes By," in film
30 Hold the floor
31 Scoundrels' society?
34 Subway relatives
35 Get rid of
36 China's Chiang ___-shek
39 Tool used in royal gardens?
43 Without delay
46 Common ID
47 Item in a cheek pouch
48 Korean War rifle
50 Bother incessantly
51 Shea Stadium's locale?
55 Bit of seafloor flora
56 Stir
57 It's about a foot
60 Litter leaver
61 Spring sign
62 An eternity, seemingly
63 Gets darker, in a way
64 Slip
65 Wool sources

DOWN
1 "The Jackie Gleason Show" shower
2 Live and breathe
3 Court order
4 Calcutta conveyance
5 Lowlife
6 City by a lake of the same name
7 Land of literature
8 Did perfectly
9 Paroxysm
10 Quarters for shopping
11 Source of gum arabic
12 Silvery white
13 Renter
21 "Let's not forget . . ."
22 Baffin Bay hazard
23 Storybook starter
24 Pitch's partner
27 Path to poverty, with "the"
28 Starting stakes
29 Georgia city
32 Org. that may request a recall
33 TV band
36 Has the skill
37 Pearl Mosque locale
38 Fails to be
39 Some iconic gems
40 Shut (up)
41 Xanadu resident
42 New Testament miracle cry
43 In shock
44 Spanish dish
45 Whence Catherine
49 Home of the Blue Monster golf course
50 Symbols of silliness
52 Roman meeting places
53 Leno line
54 Swiss army knives have several
58 Lunchtime, perhaps
59 Suffix with seer

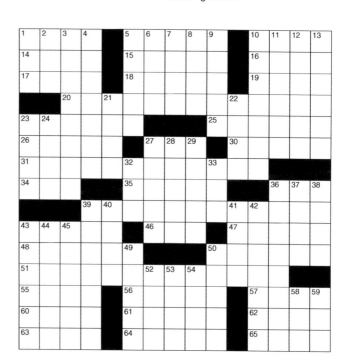

by William Schaub

ACROSS

1 Spanish eyes
5 Jots
10 News anchor Paula
14 Hitchcock title
15 Black-necked goose
16 Award started by the Village Voice
17 Reducing the autopsy staff?
20 Crime for which one takes the heat
21 Barely flows
22 Captain of science fiction
25 Alias
26 Jokester
29 Dyed trick-or-treat costume?
35 Emotionally charged
37 Subject for il poeta
38 ___-Honey (candy name)
39 High-hats
42 Ovaltine ingredient
43 People travel only one way on them
45 Permanent spot on a dress
47 Lively state?
50 Spotter
51 Prefect ending
52 Knock off
54 Growing post-W.W. II environs
59 Swing and a miss
63 Politician on a spree?
66 Pipsqueak
67 Many a McDonald's promotion
68 Stuff on slides
69 "Vamoose!"
70 Famous bucktoothed dummy
71 Longtime Susan Lucci quest

DOWN

1 Sea World attraction
2 Day at the Louvre
3 Decides
4 Decided about
5 "Son of," in Arabic names
6 Domain name suffix
7 Public relations need
8 Parka
9 Sound, as the hour
10 Stupefy, slangily
11 Explorer Tasman
12 Engage
13 Role for Stack and Costner
18 Like helium
19 City SSE of Gainesville
23 They lap France's coasts
24 God who gave up an eye to drink from the spring of wisdom
26 Home entertainment option
27 Way out
28 Imply
30 Ambit
31 Literary matchmaker
32 Warty jumpers
33 Fourth deck of a ship
34 Meshlike
36 Mrs. Dithers in "Blondie"
40 Cranberries thrive here
41 Place on a schedule
44 Bad etiquette at the dinner table
46 Famous
48 Flies around
49 Curb
53 Part of growing up
54 Estonia et al., once: Abbr.
55 Nope
56 Rock star with many causes
57 Machinating
58 Onetime Mets slugger Tommie
60 Particular
61 1040, for one
62 Scuffle
64 Hardly an ordinary Joe
65 Apt answer for this clue

by Cathy Millhauser

ACROSS

1 Diplomat Deane
6 Lancia competitor, for short
10 Tee off
14 Prepared to be dubbed
15 Cash in Qom
16 1950's British P.M.
17 Advice to a driver, part 1
20 Hardly genteel
21 Court feat
22 Hardly genteel
23 Literary monogram
24 ___ Park (Manhattan neighborhood)
27 Barcelona title
29 One-in-a-million
30 Botanist Gray
33 Advice, part 2
37 Clear of the sea bottom
40 Moulin Rouge performance
41 Advice, part 3
45 Buck's mate
46 Long story
47 Reasons to cram
51 Garden ornamentals
54 Beer may be on it
55 Waters on stage
58 Polo Grounds legend
59 "Dumb" comics girl
60 End of the advice
64 Director Rohmer
65 Tech support caller
66 Actress Anne
67 "Why not?!"
68 Nuclear fuel holders
69 Mountain nymph

DOWN

1 Evades
2 Imbue (with)
3 Dutch cheese
4 Lotion ingredient
5 1950's–70's senator Symington, for short
6 Small toucan
7 One of the front four
8 500-pound, say
9 Apiece, in scores
10 Put in hot oil again
11 Brainchild
12 "Why not?!"
13 Son of Seth
18 "This means ___!"
19 Watchdog agcy. beginning 1887
24 Some shorthand
25 Pitching stat
26 React violently, in a way

28 Final notice
30 Sector boundary
31 Rwy. stop
32 Writer Rand
34 Write for another
35 Clotho and others
36 Jet black
37 Tag on
38 A suitor may pitch it
39 Suffix with ethyl
42 Mer contents
43 Disregarded
44 Skier's leggings
48 A.S.A.P.
49 First first lady
50 Neutered
51 British coppers
52 Bridge guru Culbertson
53 J.D. holder: Abbr.
55 Farm females
56 Like some traffic

57 One who's got it coming
59 Shy creature
61 Start of many a Catholic church name
62 G.I. entertainer
63 Telephone interrogatory

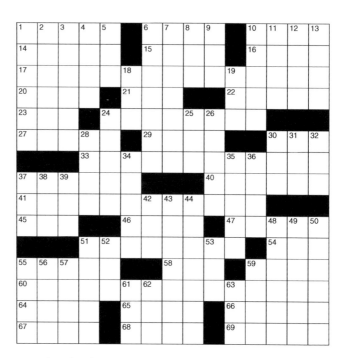

by Ed Early

ACROSS

1 RCA product
4 Rock singer/poet Smith
9 Drink from fermented milk
14 Pension supplement, for short
15 Fake fat brand
16 Rust, e.g.
17 Tribe related to the Fox
18 Civil War side
19 Gentleman's gentleman
20 Start of a definition of television, by 9-Down
23 Spendthrift's outing
24 Diplomat's asset
25 Some coll. exams
29 Feared flier
33 Definition, part 2
37 One with a list?
38 NATO member
39 Public image
42 Chi. setting
43 Buster?
45 Definition, part 3
47 Stopper, informally
50 "___ the Top"
51 Sit on it
53 Sit on it
57 End of the definition
63 Like ___ from the blue
64 Beatles phenomenon, e.g.
65 Tend the turf
66 He once worked for Edison
67 Follow, as a tip
68 Downed a sub?
69 Wood finish
70 Nary a soul
71 Aussie outlaw Kelly

DOWN

1 Travelers' papers
2 Writer's woe
3 Soap Box Derby entrant
4 Pays what is due
5 Baseball family name
6 Five to ten, e.g.
7 Makes lace
8 ___ water
9 Big name in early TV
10 Grandly praised
11 Plug
12 ___ fixe
13 No longer in the service: Abbr.
21 Crème ___ crème
22 Subject of a B. Kliban drawing
26 Enzyme suffix
27 Garr of "Young Frankenstein"
28 Hardly macho
30 Word with high- or low-
31 MS. enclosure
32 ___'acte
33 "Nonsense!"
34 Actor Morales
35 Engine part, for short
36 ___ avail
40 Opposite of alt, in German
41 727, e.g.
44 Violinist/composer Arcangelo ___
46 Prepared to drive, with "up"
48 Summer shade
49 Wellness grp.
52 Spin doctor
54 Eternal City dweller
55 Large bill
56 Cut down
57 "Phooey!"
58 Be a lookout for, say
59 Montgomery's Parks
60 City named for an Indian tribe
61 Within: Prefix
62 Big 22-Down

by Paula Gamache

ACROSS

1 "___ long story"
5 Where the Vikings landed
9 Seder serving
14 ___-a-brac
15 Heaps
16 CH-, e.g.
17 Character in "The Wizard of Oz-trich"?
19 Nursery V.I.P.
20 Happens repeatedly
21 By and by
23 Cowpoke's nickname
24 Scarcity
26 Tech course
28 Playwright Jones
30 Out for the night
34 Tight spot
37 Sir Francis Drake's Indian ship?
39 Corn product
41 June honoree
42 City on the Rhine
43 A whale of a 60's singer?
48 Two cents worth
49 Rated XXX
50 Signs of the future
52 As soon as
54 Hilarious person
57 "Sketches by ___" (1836 book)
60 Show's partner
62 Paesano's land
64 African antelope
66 Bill of fare at Rick's?
68 Formal fabric
69 Wrapped up
70 Use a beeper
71 Hoisting device
72 Sprays
73 Pun conclusion

DOWN

1 Construction piece
2 Made even
3 Because
4 Real
5 Orchestra leader
6 Kensington quaff
7 Capital of 62-Across
8 Double's job
9 Hardly feminine
10 Literary scraps
11 Windshield option
12 Postal delivery area
13 Cameo stone
18 Discount rack abbr.
22 Algerian port
25 Wrestler's arsenal
27 Smooth-tongued
29 Spud spot
31 Biblical patriarch
32 Best of the theater
33 Insignificant
34 Slugger Canseco
35 Orchard no-no
36 Staff note
38 Dutch exports
40 Camp Swampy canine
44 Suggesting indirectly
45 "___ homo" (declaration in John 19:5)
46 Occupations
47 Agreement
51 Philatelist's collection
53 Kind of room
55 Sports shoe attachment
56 Pivotal point
57 Order (around)
58 Spoken
59 Rigatoni relative
61 It means nothing to some people
63 Teacher of Heifetz
65 Hopper
67 Figure out

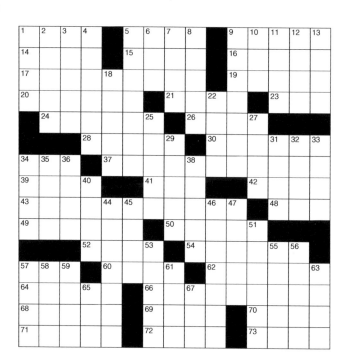

by Richard Silvestri

ACROSS

1 Italian autos
6 Jack's companion, in rhyme
10 Country bumpkin
14 Model Everhart
15 Conception
16 Addict
17 Run after a comic?
19 Litigant
20 Long, long time
21 Small amount
22 Natural gas ingredient
24 Impaled
26 In a stall, as a horse
27 Wide shoe specification
28 Kama ___
29 Maniacs
32 Chemical suffix
33 Byway
37 Sophisticated military plane
38 Big expense for newspapers
39 Pre-PC counters
40 The two of them
41 N.Y.C. line
42 Stir
43 "Thriller" singer's nickname
45 "This means ___!"
46 Fixes, as a shoe
49 Driveway endings
53 Tennis star Gibson
54 Saharalike
55 Sight from Lucerne
56 Take a dogleg, e.g.
57 Hurt a politician's wife?
60 Paradise
61 ___ Stanley Gardner
62 Nonnuclear family member
63 Wet, as morning grass
64 Any day now
65 "Beau ___"

DOWN

1 Confronts
2 ___ water (up the creek)
3 Guam's capital, old-style
4 "___ the season to be jolly"
5 Hothouse features
6 Islamic crusade
7 Alter ___ (exact duplicate)
8 "My Name Is Asher ___"
9 Newborn's paraphernalia
10 Hurry an actress along?
11 Ordinary
12 Designer Geoffrey
13 Blew it
18 Canadian Indians
23 Blacken
25 Make a baseball player sit out the game?
26 Submerged
28 ___ Domingo
29 Just great
30 ___ Jima
31 "Dig in!"
34 "Red" or "white" tree
35 Bandage brand
36 Cacophony
38 Ticks off
39 Presenter's task
41 Deep freezes, so to speak
42 Hang around for
44 Pub brew
46 Scored
47 Get away from
48 Throw here and there
49 Verdant
50 Stares
51 Vote in
52 Bender
54 Folk singer Guthrie
58 Tijuana gold
59 Crusty one?

by Stephanie Spadaccini

26

ACROSS
1 Sports column?
5 Standard deviation symbol
10 War fare?
14 Like many a hurricane
15 Allege in defense
16 Coat or skirt preceder
17 Disappointing election results
19 Seasoned
20 Help
21 Equal
22 Channeled
23 Resolute advice to the hesitant
27 Stuff for surfacing
28 He's found in the Prado
29 Community contest
30 Stumpers?
33 Flags
34 Hal Foster comic character
35 One associated with honesty
36 No one special
38 Castilian hero
39 Expert on the rules
40 Good relations
41 Manages, with "out"
42 N.Y. minutes?
43 Fountain in New Orleans
44 Word for word: Abbr.
46 1985 sequel to a classic 1939 film
48 Donny or Marie Osmond, e.g.
51 Unit of nautical displacement
52 Tall topper
54 Gee
56 Like bats
58 Biblical book
59 Available
60 Small animal shelter

61 Short time out?
62 They follow cuts
63 Dict. offering

DOWN
1 First name in animation
2 "This __ Youth" (Kenneth Lonergan play)
3 Just learning about
4 Discovery of Galileo
5 Comparatively quick
6 Long series of woes
7 Lee, e.g.: Abbr.
8 __ wheel
9 Plugs
10 Burn
11 Gripping read
12 Brutally destroy

13 Season opener?
18 Miss, south of the border
21 Parsley relative
23 Fine accompaniment?
24 Promise, e.g.
25 À la Poe
26 Fractures
28 Exile of 1302
30 Kitchen gizmo
31 Really big
32 Rights shouldn't be taken from it
33 Frosty
36 No performers are found here
37 Red sky, maybe
41 Colorize, e.g.
44 Immerses
45 Draper's unit
47 Cad
48 Slight indication?

49 "What __!" ("Hilarious!")
50 Like some habits
52 Numerical prefix
53 Overflow
54 Modicum
55 Insurance letters
56 Green-light indicator
57 Person

by James M. and James C. Jenista

As a demonstration of speed puzzle construction at the 28th American Crossword Puzzle Tournament, on March 11 in Stamford, Conn., Mike Shenk took a theme proposed by the audience and created this puzzle, start to finish, without computer-assisted fill, in 60 minutes. Later, in a race to solve it, Trip Payne, of Boca Raton, Fla., finished first, in 3 minutes. About two-thirds of the audience completed the puzzle correctly within the 15-minute time limit.

ACROSS

1 Desert flora
6 Coated candy
11 Interstice
14 Wolf pack member
15 Without company
16 Outback runner
17 Vegetarian tennis star?
19 Surfing site
20 They're underfoot
21 All in
23 Greet the opposing team
26 Vanna's partner
27 Gets along
29 Tibias' ends
31 Culminating point
32 Femme fatale
33 Choral work
34 Doc bloc, for short
37 Volunteer's words
38 Bone connector
39 Thick cut
40 Kareem, once
41 Misanthrope
42 Roberts of "Mystic Pizza"
43 Camera card contents
45 Mass parts
46 Sunday paper section
48 Memorial Day setting
49 Course start
50 Bound to experience
51 Goes belly-up
53 Rockies tree
54 Vegetarian film critic?
60 Popular season on the Riviera
61 Drove to distraction
62 Austin Powers's father
63 Curious George creator H. A. ___

64 Demands
65 Sharpshooting Shaq

DOWN

1 New reporter
2 Penny portrait
3 Runner Sebastian
4 Does a doily
5 Answer to a knock
6 "American Buffalo" playwright
7 Yodelers' milieu
8 Hide-hair link
9 Modern evidence
10 Camper's gear
11 Vegetarian film critic?
12 Change the Constitution
13 Tie up a boat
18 Sighed cry
22 Sulky state
23 Pesto base

24 In reserve
25 Vegetarian talk show star?
27 Poet's concern
28 Fresh
30 Cariou of "Sweeney Todd"
31 Shipping areas
33 Itty-bitty bugs
35 L.L. Bean's home
36 Lower
38 Wise fellow
39 Catch some rays
41 Kind of turn
42 "Leading With My Chin" author
44 6 on a phone
45 First born?
46 Drummer's partner
47 Bring together
48 Hotel staffers
51 Hightailed it
52 It's got you covered

55 Beatitudes verb
56 Island strings
57 Epoch
58 Salonga of "Miss Saigon"
59 Wing

by Mike Shenk

28

ACROSS

1 "Just ___"
5 Kodak rival
9 Put away
14 Vaquero's view
15 Show off, like Mr. America
16 Product first used commercially in toothbrush bristles
17 ___ Sea, outlet for the Amu Darya
18 Honest
19 Polish
20 See circles
23 Road hazard in Frankfurt
24 Doesn't bother
28 See circles
34 One of the sons on "My Three Sons"
35 Friedrich ___, first president of the German Republic
36 Univ. applicants, typically
37 Kitchen canful
38 U.S. military planes
39 Substitute position
40 "Lord, is ___?"
41 Subjects of research, e.g.
42 Sun block
43 See circles
46 Title words repeated in a 1974 song after "Como una promesa . . ."
47 Monte Leone, for one
48 See circles
55 "When it comes to . . ."
58 Leave
59 Prefix with knock or lock
60 "The Price Is Right" announcement
61 Indian melodic pattern
62 Poker declaration

63 Last-minute birthday recognition
64 Big name in theaters?
65 Lean

DOWN

1 Key of Beethoven's Symphony No. 7: Abbr.
2 Hospital fluids
3 Actor Morales
4 Modern means of character recognition?
5 From the top
6 Dale
7 Guinness entry
8 Toll unit
9 Minimal postage hike
10 M.L.B. team with a bridge in its logo
11 Land in un fleuve
12 Swindle
13 Dissolve
21 Part of the cyberworld
22 10-Down, e.g.
25 Affirmative in the lyrics of "Penny Serenade"
26 Concerned
27 Check again
28 One of five Spanish kings
29 Sen. Robert Byrd, for one
30 Green
31 Stop, perhaps
32 Steel bar
33 Mind-set?
38 Housewives, abroad
39 Female rocker with the 2003 hit "Why Can't I?"
41 Spayed

42 Actor Kilmer and others
44 What a B'way show might have
45 Big source of state revenue
49 Actress Austin
50 Final, say
51 Gulf of ___, arm of the Baltic
52 "Lean ___"
53 Certain Monopoly sq.
54 Peewee
55 Many a Monopoly sq.
56 Cyst
57 Its state flower is the orange blossom: Abbr.

by Michael Shteyman

ACROSS

1 Corday's victim
6 Billiard shot
11 Convenience store sign
14 Classic game company
15 Like World Cup crowds
16 Charles X, e.g.
17 59-Across and others
19 Dispenser of 47-Across
20 Irritate
21 Where to spend kips
22 Mid fourth-century year
24 Results of ties: Abbr.
25 ___-Hawley Tariff Act of 1930
26 Cheer
27 Shelley's "___ Skylark"
28 Old Chevy
31 Professional grp.
34 Comment made while fanning oneself
37 Cyclades island
38 Classic Dickens title (from whose 10 letters this puzzle was constructed)
41 ___ polloi
42 Itsy bits
43 Must
44 Casual walk
46 Show
47 See 19-Across
48 Commandment word
51 ___ Poly
54 Wreck
56 Sail supporter
57 Colombian city
58 Coach Parseghian
59 Ebenezer Scrooge player in a 1951 movie version of 38-Across

62 ___ chi ch'uan
63 Conductor Georg
64 Portuguese colony until 1999
65 Entirely
66 Kind of energy
67 Pile up

DOWN

1 Introduction to economics?
2 On ___ (carousing)
3 "Groundhog Day" director
4 Seed covering
5 Start of a winning combination
6 Major export of Ivory Coast
7 Movie droid, familiarly
8 Perch
9 Stick in the water

10 Tiny Tim's mother in 38-Across
11 Places for theorizers?
12 Shed item
13 Rodolfo's love in "La Bohème"
18 ___ mater
23 Suffix with mini or Web
25 Working poor, e.g., in 38-Across
27 Rocky hill
28 1980's–90's TV nickname
29 Cheer (for)
30 Kon-Tiki Museum site
31 Cries of delight
32 59-Across, e.g.
33 It's usually tucked in
34 "Am ___ believe . . . ?"
35 "Dee-lish!"
36 Joke responses

39 Cards, on the scoreboard
40 Berne's river
45 Commercial suffix with Rock
46 Utah ski resort
48 Trivial
49 "___ mañana"
50 Moving
51 Conspirator against Caesar
52 Popular spy show
53 Line at an airport
54 "Bye now"
55 Spoken
57 Jampack
60 John
61 "Well, ___ monkey's uncle!"

by David J. Kahn

ACROSS

1 Join rudely, as a conversation
7 Pantry lineup
11 Consume
14 Big and muscular
15 Genesis brother
16 Org. awarding cultural grants
17 2 cups . . .
19 Make a sharp turn
20 Wahine's wreath
21 Old Italian bread
22 Label info
23 Prefix with mature
25 1/2 cup . . .
28 Catches
30 Grp. with the 1976 hit "Livin' Thing"
31 Biol. subject
32 Ticklee's cry
35 Longtime Mell Lazarus comic strip
39 . . . to taste
42 ___ nous
43 Chamber stock
44 Greeting in London's East End
45 Howe'er
47 Passed out
49 3/4 teaspoon . . .
54 Abilene-to-San Antonio dir.
55 Go here and there
56 Nest site
57 Balancing pro, in brief
59 Egg head?
60 1 teaspoon . . .
64 According to
65 Gulf war ally
66 Texas oil city
67 Operating with ulterior motives
68 Word before come and go
69 Something to be hoist by

DOWN

1 ___ America (cable TV service)
2 Country between Braz. and Arg.
3 3/4 teaspoon . . . .
4 Oh-so-quaint, in England
5 Rainbow shade
6 Big inits. in newspapers
7 Farr or Foxx
8 Can't hit the broad side of ___
9 Record over
10 Traffic caution
11 Decompress, as a computer file
12 Collar
13 Not just ready
18 Pseudo fat
22 Reverend credited with saying "The Lord is a shoving leopard"
23 Better than show
24 Arrested
26 Break
27 "Sesame Street" character with a goldfish named Dorothy
29 Make the hair stand on end
33 Start of a tuba sound
34 Having a scented ointment, as hair
36 What 17-, 25-, 39-, 49- and 60-Across and 3-Down combine to make
37 Tunnelers
38 Cell terminal
40 Classic soft drink
41 Investment firm T. ___ Price
46 Ideals
48 It comes with all the bells and whistles
49 Wheat and corn
50 Shanty
51 Shade of white
52 SeaWorld attractions
53 Pipsqueak
58 ___-à-porter
60 Where the buck stops?
61 Org. that's in the red?
62 Syr. neighbor
63 Jerk

by Patrick Blindauer

ACROSS

1 Didn't take advantage of
9 Muscleheaded
15 He conducted the premiere performances of "Pagliacci" and "La Bohème"
17 Bands of holy men
18 Become one
19 Newspaper column separators
20 ___ Elliot, heroine of Jane Austen's "Persuasion"
21 Star of "Gigi" and "Lili"
22 Put on an unhappy face
23 Revival movement's leader?
24 Strand at the airport, maybe
25 Maker of Coolpix cameras
26 Stray animals don't have them
27 ___ Couple (yearbook voting category)
28 "Field of Dreams" actress Amy
31 1979 #1 hit for Robert John
32 More of the same
33 Like St. Basil's
34 Incite
35 Center
36 Yielding ground
39 Young cowboy in "Lonesome Dove"
40 Ships on the seafloor
41 Roofing choice
42 Compliant
44 Gives up responsibility
45 Sometime soon
47 One with a guitar and shades, stereotypically
48 Bathe in a glow
49 Most mawkish

DOWN

1 Game featuring Blinky, Pinky, Inky and Clyde
2 Photographer/ children's author Alda
3 Jelly seen on buffet tables
4 Kind of protector
5 Pennsylvania's Flagship City
6 Vet, e.g.
7 Stage actress who wrote "Respect for Acting"
8 Pilot light?
9 Treat badly
10 Albee's "Three ___ Women"
11 Vast
12 One that gets depressed during recitals
13 Awaiting burial
14 Files a minority opinion
16 Boxy Toyota product
21 Some emergency cases may be found in them
24 Steely Dan singer Donald
25 Some Degas paintings
26 1939 film taglined "Garbo laughs"
27 First African-born Literature Nobelist
28 "Is There Life Out There" singer
29 Titular mouse in a classic Daniel Keyes novel
30 1600 to 1800, on a boat
31 Big hit
33 Number to the left of a decimal point, maybe
35 Unlikely to rattle or squeak, say
36 Trifling
37 Political extremists
38 Roughly a third of the earth's land surface
40 Carthaginian statesman who opposed war with Rome
41 Rwandan people
43 Blue shade
44 Great literature's opposite
46 Possible work force reducer

by Patrick Berry

ACROSS

1 France's ___ von Bismarck
5 Jumped
11 Rogue
14 Chemical element with the symbol Fe
15 Sub
16 Discounted item: Abbr.
17 Gets it wrong
18 Terrible one?
19 Former pharmaceutical giant
20 Flow slowly
21 Flat things?
22 Out of: Ger.
23 Sum derives from it
24 Father of Jacob
25 Monopoly quartet: Abbr.
26 Spot
31 Preemie setting: Abbr.
32 Suffix with palm
33 Collection of teams
36 Crane, e.g.
39 Possible name for the first decade of the century
40 Hold back
41 Hardly soothes
42 Former Romanian leader Ion ___
43 One step from the majors
44 Nickname on the Houston Rockets starting in 2004
45 Kind of dog
51 Solution strength: Abbr.
52 Road access regulators
53 Sooner
54 Always bouncing back
55 Places for La-Z-Boys
56 Number of clues in this puzzle that contain factual inaccuracies
57 Dwarf planet larger than Pluto

DOWN

1 "I'll be with you shortly . . ."
2 Mother of Calcutta
3 One way to lay things
4 Uncommissioned
5 Silverstein who wrote and illustrated "The Giving Tree"
6 Corn dish
7 San ___, Calif.
8 Golf great Andre
9 Standard office-closing time
10 Arises
11 One who exhibits pack mentality?
12 Who quipped "God tells me how the music should sound, but you stand in the way"
13 Job seeker's fashion advice
27 Bolt
28 It's more than 90 degrees
29 "Nope, still not right"
30 Writing that's hard to read
33 Mill input
34 Part of E.E.C.: Abbr.
35 Turkish pooh-bah
36 Verdi's "___ tu"
37 Th.D. subj.
38 Prefix with center
45 Narrow passage: Abbr.
46 Job ad abbr.
47 Tennis champ Ernie
48 Time to lie in le soleil?
49 Currency of China
50 Summer hrs. in N.Y.C.

by Joe Krozel

ACROSS

1 Vis-à-vis
16 Age-old retaliation
17 Having no inaccuracy whatsoever
18 "___ say . . ."
19 Necklace decoration
20 Alicante article
21 Crime scene evidence, often
26 Peau de ___ (soft fabric)
27 Old TV ministry
28 Automated, often malicious PC apps
30 Slangy suffix
31 Fix things
34 Dramatic break
35 A firefighter at work may be in it
41 First suit?
42 Robin Goodfellow and others
43 "Blood hath been shed ___ now": Macbeth
44 Isn't right on
46 Author Madame de ___
47 It's a ball
48 Compete for, in a way
50 ___ please
51 James Ellroy novel that Time magazine named best fiction book of 1995
57 Suitable for all
58 Idolizes

DOWN

1 Fast-food restaurant packets
2 Italian port with ruins of an imposing Aragonese castle
3 Longtime Arizona congressman who ran for president in 1976
4 People who deal with stress successfully?
5 Quintillionth: Prefix
6 Pythagorean character
7 Bog youngster
8 Bart Simpson hears it a lot
9 Be transformed?
10 Miss at a barn dance
11 Amenhotep IV's god
12 Shreds
13 "That's hardly amusing"
14 Not being productive
15 Time for an emergency phone call?
21 They may break open cases
22 Inside
23 Torpor
24 Opposite of scanty
25 Cobbler alternative
28 Compromises
29 Things kept behind bars
32 Be in the running
33 TV bear
35 Swelling reducers
36 Writer whose novella "Carmen" is the basis of Bizet's opera
37 Musical ornament using two quickly alternating tones
38 "La Traviata" lover Alfredo ___
39 Section of some bookstores
40 Give a face-lift
45 Dressing targets
47 A ton
49 De ___ (Nolte's "Cape Fear" co-star)
50 Anne Nichols title protagonist
52 Poky
53 According to
54 Occasion to recharge
55 Shrovetide concluder: Abbr.
56 Do a summer's work?

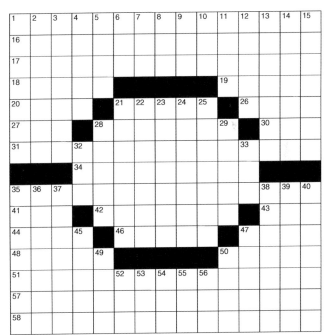

by Frank Longo

ACROSS
1 Turkish __
5 Dutch __
10 Like horses' hooves
14 Bush not seen much nowadays
15 Toward the Arctic
16 Sioux City's locale
17 Lampblack
18 Measure of prevention or strength?
19 Superheroes battling the evil Magneto
20 Russian __
22 Swiss __
24 Now and again
25 Military pooh-bahs
26 Preceders of xis
27 Buck's tail?
28 Cap with a pompom
31 Semicircular building extension
34 Australian __
35 American __
36 Light wood
38 The Buckeyes, for short
39 Skirt
41 Italian __
42 Canadian __
44 Union agreements?
45 Golf peg
46 Scientologist Hubbard
47 Hill, in Haifa
49 Spanish verse
51 Operatic movement circa 1900
55 Danish __
57 Portuguese __
58 Very much
59 Appetite stimulant
61 Collector's suffix
62 Place to order a sandwich or espresso
63 Sturdy chiffon
64 Put out
65 Ivan or Feodor
66 French __
67 Spanish __

DOWN
1 Iraqi seaport
2 Going on
3 Lake catch
4 Crisis center connections
5 Govt. securities
6 Licks soundly
7 White-tailed eagle
8 Takeoff and landing overseers: Abbr.
9 Brandon Lee's last movie
10 Boxcars
11 Locale for a pioneer family
12 Is in the red
13 Hamlet, e.g.
21 Part of the Australian coat of arms
23 Outlander in Hawaii
25 Brand of razors and coffee makers
27 Burning issue
29 Fashion designer Gucci
30 Ladies of Versailles: Abbr.
31 Not much
32 Double time, for one
33 Convertible
34 Après-ski drink
37 Better trained
40 Slanderer
43 Tiny marcher
47 Kind of farmer
48 Leandro's partner in a Mancinelli opera
50 Prized fur
51 "Let's go, amigo!"
52 Hindu wise one
53 Bouncing off the walls
54 Speak before throngs
55 Agreement
56 "'Tis a pity"
57 Lisa with a "mystic smile"
60 Grande opening?

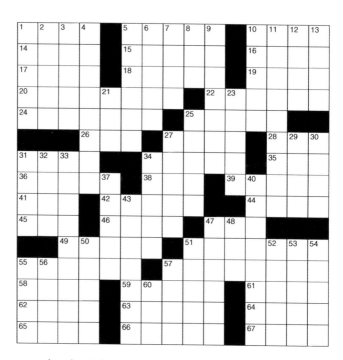

by John Underwood

ACROSS

1 Frog-dissecting class: Abbr.
5 "Ship of Fools" painter
10 Riot queller
14 Pink, maybe
15 Lawn care brand
16 "Such a pity"
17 Slate, e.g.
18 Where was the Battle of Bunker Hill fought?
20 Makes invalid
22 California Indian tribe: Var.
23 Seminary teaching
24 Drain
25 Cousin of a cat's-eye
29 What animal does a bulldogger throw?
30 Drop ___ (moon)
32 Soprano Gluck
33 Get copy right
35 Money
37 In what country are Panama hats made?
41 What is George Eliot's given name?
42 It'll keep the home fires burning
43 Queens's ___ Stadium
44 Seed cover
45 Golfer Ballesteros
47 From what animals do we get catgut?
52 Smallest
54 Soft shoe, briefly
55 Part of São Paulo
56 Column style
58 Putting up the greatest affront
59 In what country are Chinese gooseberries produced?
63 Times to call, in some want ads
64 Unoccupied
65 Deejay's interest, typically
66 Port opener?
67 Family dogs, for short
68 Very funny happenings
69 The "I" in M.I.T.: Abbr.

DOWN

1 Challah and baguettes
2 "You are so!" preceder
3 What color is the black box in a commercial jet?
4 Pea, for one
5 Short cuts
6 Bruins' retired "4"
7 What is actor Stewart Granger's family name?
8 For next to nothing, in slang
9 Brick carriers
10 Reddish brown
11 Clay, today
12 "Silent" prez
13 Adult ed. class, often
19 ___ Na Na
21 Rio Grande port
24 Recipe verb
26 "M*A*S*H" star
27 Eliot Ness and others
28 Bring home
31 The California gull is the state bird of which state?
34 For what animals are the Canary Islands named?
36 1974 Mocedades hit
37 Not différent
38 ___ package
39 Former Voice of America org.
40 Nobody too big or too small, on a sign
41 Fraction of a tick: Abbr.
43 What kind of fruit is an alligator pear?
46 Actor Estevez
48 Cab Calloway phrase
49 How many colleges were once in the Big Ten?
50 Ford failures
51 Take care of a neighbor's dog, say
53 Piggy
57 He wrote "If called by a panther, / Don't anther"
58 Nutritional amts.
59 Cowboys' org.
60 Cold war ___
61 Site for a site
62 Site for a site

by Ed Stein and Paula Gamache

ACROSS

1 Source of the line "Frailty, thy name is woman!"
7 Some believers
13 Poor thing about a slouch
14 Vacation destinations
16 Dressed for a white-tie affair
17 Order in the court
18 Some urban digs
19 Shooter on the playground
21 Old Al Capp strip "___ an' Slats"
22 He preceded Joan at Woodstock
23 Former org. protecting depositors
25 Water collector
26 Mens ___ (criminal intent)
27 One who is no longer entitled
29 Golf club part
30 Set off, in a big way
32 Bigger-than-life persona
34 & 35 With 35-Across, one who has done the circled things, combined, more often than any other major-league player
36 Attempts to strike
39 Georgia birthplace of Erskine Caldwell
43 Want ad abbr.
44 Cheese dish
46 Hotel addition?
47 U.S.N. brass: Abbr.
49 Photographic flash gas
50 Latin wings
51 Lab tube
53 Action stopper
54 "Can ___ Witness" (Marvin Gaye hit)
55 ___ Sánchez, co-director of "The Blair Witch Project"
57 Turned a blind eye toward
59 Last of the French?
60 Lemonlike fruit
61 Spoke rudely to
62 Classic brand of liniment

DOWN

1 Mother, on the second Sunday in May
2 Whence Elaine, in Arthurian lore
3 Highest peak in the Philippines: Abbr.
4 Baseball All-Star Tiant
5 Goethe's "The ___- King"
6 Where to take an exam
7 Attract
8 Fish that may be caught in a cage
9 Puerto Rico, por ejemplo
10 Gathers on a surface, chemically
11 Reason for a medley, perhaps
12 Apostle called "the Zealot"
13 Enterprise-D captain
15 Permeated, with "into"
20 On the safe side
23 Political proposal from some conservatives
24 Fill, as with a crayon
27 Lend ___
28 Kind of button
31 Special ___
33 Breast enlargement material
35 Branch of technology
36 Like some spoonfuls
37 Salt add-ins
38 Japanese restaurant offering
39 Restaurant offering
40 Bank controller
41 Tidies
42 Rastafarian's do, for short
45 34 & 35-Across's 4,256 career hits, e.g.
48 Penn and others
50 Pythagoras' square
52 Speaker of the diamond
54 Digging
56 Near failure
58 Apt name for an ichthyologist?

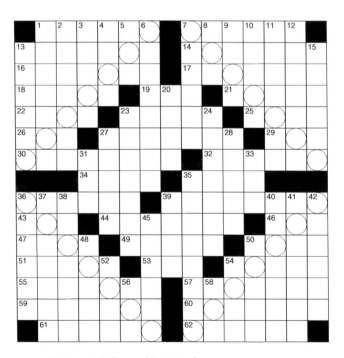

by Peter A. Collins and Joe Krozel

ACROSS

1 Facility
5 ← What this is, on a calendar
8 Signals
12 Jiltee of myth
14 Yamaha offering, in brief
15 Perform acceptably
16 Profanities (and a hint to this puzzle's anomalies)
19 Peer group?
20 Razz
21 Liverpool-to-Portsmouth dir.
23 Buzzers
25 Some exchanges, quickly
28 Arrives
30 Mean mien
32 Scale range
33 Do what Jell-O does
34 Alley of Moo
35 Patient responses
36 Geisha's accessory
37 Like
38 Many "Star Wars" fighters
40 Blood, e.g.
42 Forward
43 Some people in a tree
44 Division of an office bldg.
45 Wasn't straight
46 Carry-___
47 Garden sights
49 Is behind
51 Record holders? (and a punny hint to this puzzle's anomalies)
58 Sluggish
59 Whistle blower
60 "American Idol" judge
61 "Man oh man!"
62 ___ admin (computer techie)
63 Hip

DOWN

1 Voltaic cell meas.
2 Abbr. in a help-wanted ad
3 E-mail address ending
4 Like H. P. Lovecraft among all popular writers?
5 Show types
6 Part of a 2005 SBC merger
7 Actress Mimieux of "Where the Boys Are"
8 Offering, as a price
9 12 or 15 min.
10 Rx abbr.
11 Peck parts: Abbr.
13 Iranian supreme leader ___ Khamenei
15 100 lbs.
17 Some musical notes
18 Football linemen: Abbr.
21 They may have niños and niñas
22 Exit
24 Royal son of the comics
26 Nuclear unit
27 Merchants
28 Stuff on a shelf
29 Kowtower
30 Squeals
31 Cans
33 Courtroom identification
36 Starts of some sporting events
39 Big chip off the old block?
40 Health supplement chain
41 Defended
43 Pergolas
45 Dance grp. at the Met
48 It goes over a plate
50 ___ leash
51 Horse and buggy
52 Official lang. of Barbados
53 Part of a violin
54 Hardly macho
55 Actress Williams of the 1960s–'70s
56 ___ Lopez (chess opening)
57 On the ___

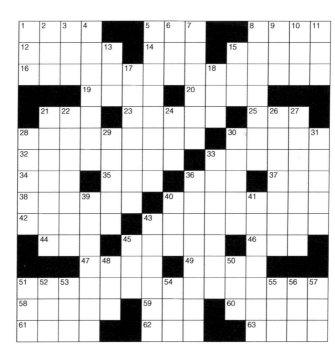

by Ashish Vengsarkar

38

ACROSS

1 Wood cutters
8 Small river craft: Var.
15 Psychiatrist's arsenal
17 They were used on old TV's "Twenty One"
18 Welcome things on hectic workdays
19 Concluding notes
20 Start making a stink?
21 Increase in volume, in mus.
22 Zapped
23 Modern, in Münster
24 Timor Sea, vis-à-vis the Indian Ocean
25 Sank on a course
26 Little wood
27 Well-thought-out
29 Kind of network
30 They have their limits
31 Freshener since the 1890s
32 Economical way to buy
33 Punch-Out!! maker
35 "___ beauty, so to speak, nor good talk . . .": Kipling
36 Styles
37 It might get a plug
38 Ravel's "Ma Mère ___," a k a "Mother Goose"
39 Model's series
40 Bond variety, briefly
41 Little or wee follower
42 Restaurant opener?
43 Late, in León
44 Process associated with socialism
47 Having no pressing needs?
48 Service staples
49 Annoyances

DOWN

1 Part of a track team?
2 Rebel
3 Long-disproven scientific theory
4 Framework components
5 Some prosecutors: Abbr.
6 Not ideal for a picnic
7 Sponge skeleton parts
8 ___ knee
9 "That's just ___!"
10 Chinese menu possessive
11 Asian way
12 Launching a start-up, say
13 Number of nights in old stories
14 Pittsburgh giant
16 Hornswoggled
22 Small choir, maybe
23 Pointless
25 Jack, e.g.
26 Decimal point follower
28 Attack barbarously
29 Iberian infants
31 Course component
32 Out around midday, say
33 Register button
34 Breaks in
36 Toddlers cut them
39 Instrumentation location
40 Swimmer Biondi and others
42 Hitter of 66 in '98
43 Old propaganda source
45 Publisher Ballantine
46 He overthrew Bhutto

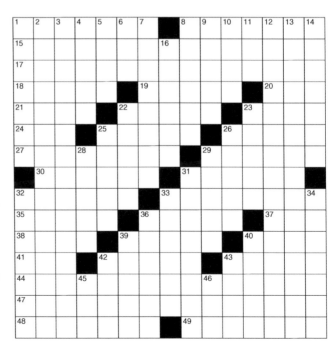

by Joe Krozel

ACROSS

1 It's similar to cream
5 *Jigger
10 Crawl (with)
14 '08 classmate, now
15 1967 war locale
16 Title heroine who says "One half of the world cannot understand the pleasures of the other"
17 *"That's way off"
19 Arabic for "commander"
20 1986 #1 hit for Starship
21 "Saving Grace" airer
23 "The Whiffenpoof Song" singer
24 Mideast's Mount ___
27 With 52-Across, wild guess . . . or what the answer to each starred clue has?
29 Nabokov novel
30 Stop on Magellan's circumnavigation of the world
32 Camera setting
33 Prefix denoting 10 to the ninth power
35 "For real!"
38 *Photo
39 *Colorful party drink
40 *Rejected
44 Pack rat
46 El número de agosto
47 FedEx, say
49 Explorer and Navigator
51 Butt
52 See 27-Across
55 Many magicians wear them
57 QB's cry

58 Solo in science fiction
59 Nonchalance
60 Sch. located on the Rio Grande
62 *Quick hitch-up
67 Maven
68 Creating a din
69 Book before Amos
70 Give a handicap of
71 *Y-shaped item
72 ___-Aryan

DOWN

1 Suffix with Euclid
2 Trapped
3 Vegetable that's peeled
4 Shadow
5 Federal management agcy.
6 Rapper ___ Jon
7 "Is that ___?"
8 Nick name?

9 Omens
10 *What "fore" may precede
11 Daniel Decatur ___, composer of "Dixie"
12 Actor Estevez
13 San Rafael's county
18 Masculine side
22 Cuisine with sen yai noodles
24 Is seconds behind
25 Spiritualist's tool
26 Whistle-blower
28 One-up
31 Pinochle combos
34 Insect called a greenfly in Britain
36 Rat Island resident
37 Red of early jazz
41 Reason to celebrate
42 Bleached
43 Often-ladled drinks
45 Mako shark prey

47 "Shhh!," not so politely
48 Straight
50 Earned a citation?
52 Some riffraff
53 Sitar pieces
54 Small ridge on the edge of a button or dial
56 Completer of the fifth pillar of Islam
61 *Track-and-field event
63 "___ won't!"
64 Pale
65 .0000001 joule
66 Mop & ___

by Joel Fagliano

40

ACROSS

1 Gulf competitor
5 "What Do You Do With ___ in English?" ("Avenue Q" song)
8 Preserved, in a way
13 Vat waste
14 Hipster
15 A Previn
16 Canaanite deity
17 Tractor make, briefly
18 More sumptuously furnished
19 No holds barred
21 Craft that's the subject of this puzzle
23 Subject of "Hofmann's Potion"
25 Finish behind
26 ___ Americano
30 Customarily
32 Physical sound
35 United hub
36 ___ Haskins, 1960s–'70s N.B.A. player
37 "___, sing America": Langston Hughes
38 Spicy sauce
39 PX, e.g.
40 Line to Penn Sta.
41 Marilyn's mark
42 Kind of board
43 It may get food away from a canine
44 Had eggs, e.g.
45 Mercury and Gemini astronaut, informally
46 Forename meaning "born again"
47 Old-fashioned "Sweet!"
49 Group of pin-heads?" Abbr.
51 How the passengers went in 21-Across
54 Brute
59 Paris's Rue de ___
60 Frank
62 National frozen dessert chain
63 Penguin from Antarctica
64 Follow relentlessly
65 Viking foe?
66 Excellence
67 Withdrawn
68 Louis VIII nickname, with "the"

DOWN

1 Hundred Days campaign planning site
2 It makes an impression
3 Navy commando
4 ___ City Hall, Nobel ceremony locale
5 Sales off. folders
6 Sound made while being fleeced?
7 Envelope abbr.
8 James of "Star Trek"
9 Allen and ___, old comedy duo
10 It fills a chest
11 Loupe user, say
12 Dagger
15 "Puh-leeze!"
20 Title role for a 1997 Oscar nominee
22 Sweet frozen treat
24 "Billy Bathgate" novelist, 1989
26 "New York, New York" has one
27 "What ___!" ("So funny!")
28 Toppled
29 Available
31 Reason for 21-Across
33 Basketball shooting game
34 Gymnast's equipment
37 "Winnie ___ Pu"
39 Certain terrier
43 Memorable 1996 hurricane
45 Works stocked by a bookstore with a rainbow flag
48 Locale in a Carlo Levi best seller
50 Loose
51 Vehicle that makes pit stops?
52 Like some loads
53 2:1, e.g.
55 "___ be all right"
56 Early 12th-century year
57 "Peek-___!"
58 "For Better or for Worse" cartoonist Johnston
61 "That's gotta hurt!"

by Francis Heaney and Patrick Blindauer

ACROSS

1 9+3+1+⅓+⅑+ . . ., e.g.
16 Dating service questionnaire heading
17 Seminal naturalistic work
18 They're dishwasher-safe
19 Main character?
20 Tree-line tree
21 Some 21-Downs
25 Tir à ___ (bow-and-arrow sport: Fr.)
27 Punch lines?
30 Thunderstorm product
31 Fit by careful shifting
32 Help in hunting
33 Routine statement?
36 ___ francese
37 Puttering
38 Fish garnish
39 Novelist who was a lifelong friend of Capote
40 Ducky
41 What the ugly duckling really was
42 Tipping point?
43 Where one might keep time?
44 Heart and brain
53 Doesn't hedge
54 A lot may be on one's mind
55 13-time Grey Cup winners

DOWN

1 Hoods may conceal them
2 German "genuine"
3 "Cup ___" (1970s Don Williams song)
4 Trend in 1970s fashion
5 "Sure, but . . ."
6 10-kilogauss units
7 Potato preparation aid
8 California's Mission Santa ___
9 Milk holders: Abbr.
10 Spares
11 Sizzling, so to speak
12 Point (to)
13 "This ___ . . . Then" (Jennifer Lopez album)
14 Citation abbreviation
15 Govt. database entries
21 One with subjects
22 Nitrogen compound
23 Physicist James who contributed to the laws of thermodynamics
24 He had a #4 hit with "It's Time to Cry"
25 Hanukkah nosh
26 Visibly horrified
27 Odysseus saw him as a shade in the underworld
28 Animated character who likes "Hello, Dolly!" songs
29 Lane pain?
31 Sci-fi's Chief Chirpa, e.g.
32 One of the Palins
34 Creator of some illusions
35 Time of awakening
40 Dan ___, 1994 Olympics speed-skating gold medalist
41 "Alistair ___ America" (1973 book)
42 Need for some shots
43 Top-___ (sports brand)
44 To be in a faraway land
45 Basis of development
46 Compliment's opposite
47 Hand ___
48 Lightman who wrote "Einstein's Dreams"
49 1958 Best Song Oscar winner
50 "Lemme ___!"
51 Chile child
52 Fleet fleet, once

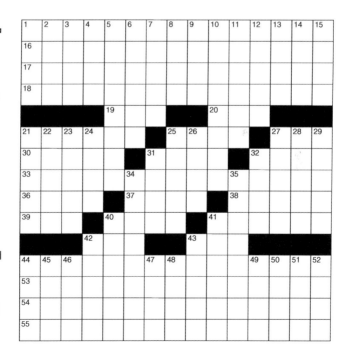

by Kevin G. Der

42

ACROSS

1 Kobe Bryant's team, on scoreboards
4 Boxing champ Hector
11 Earlier
14 Near East honorific
15 Like boot camp vis-à-vis day camp
16 Annihilate, with "down"
17 Odd sign at a Michelin dealership?
20 Roast, e.g.
21 In agreement with the group
22 Photography pioneer
26 Goes after
28 Part of an academic title
30 ___ cheese
31 The Black Stallion and others
35 Choreographer Lubovitch
36 Odd sign at Victoria's Secret?
40 Carrier to Tokyo
41 Shortcut, perhaps
42 Computer innards, for short
44 Issues
48 Like slow students, sometimes
52 Summerlike
53 Kind of disorder
55 Alphabet string
56 Odd sign at Men's Wearhouse?
60 Sch. in Brooklyn, N.Y.
61 ABC daytime staple since 1997
62 U.R.L. ending
63 Program holders
64 Extra
65 ___ Accord (1998 Mideast peace agreement)

DOWN

1 Physical expense
2 Radiant
3 Who wrote "He who does not trust enough will not be trusted"
4 Comedian Margaret
5 Jr. Olympics sponsor
6 "The A-Team" muscleman
7 Concerning
8 Popular wedding gift
9 Tea flavorings
10 Sandwiches for dessert
11 Panhandle city
12 Bookbinding decoration
13 Get behind
18 Symbol of limpness
19 Car whose name is an acronym
23 Stuck
24 ___ 2600
25 Nile Valley region
27 Roar producer
29 More than a raid
32 "Oh, give me ___ . . ."
33 Frequent spoilers
34 Grade
36 Milk: Prefix
37 For everyone to see
38 Spiral-shelled creature
39 Talents
43 Soaks (up)
45 61-Across, e.g.
46 Bistro
47 Gunk
49 One-sided contests
50 Electrical pioneer Thomson
51 Antique dealer, at times
54 Answer
56 Frequent Winter Olympics site
57 The "S" in 54-Down
58 Romanian currency
59 Jimmy Stewart syllables

by Dan Naddor

ACROSS

1 Bug detection devices?
6 Yemeni, for one
10 Red indication on a clock radio
14 O. Henry, e.g.
15 Navigational reference points
17 Answer
18 Native Australian winds
19 Davy Jones or any other Monkee
20 Relayed (to)
21 Oiler or liner
23 Bowler alternative
25 Inhabitants of central African rain forests
29 Nary a soul
30 Tun
32 Only actor to win a comedy and drama Emmy for the same character
33 Drench
34 Abba hit of 1976
36 Yossarian's tentmate in "Catch-22"
37 Wooden or metal framework
40 Implements in a coffee shop
43 Lobbies, often
44 Less leisurely
45 Ballpark fare
47 Engaged, and then some
51 Shunned shellfish, say
55 Aboard a 21-Across, maybe
56 You might get it at a nursery
57 "It Don't Come Easy" singer, 1971
58 Nautically equipped, in a way
59 Good place for a smoke
60 Incite
61 "Dawn of the ___ fingers . . .": The Odyssey
62 Opposite of hatred

DOWN

1 Final section of T. S. Eliot's "The Waste Land"
2 Brand with the slogan "All Day Strong"
3 Teen drivers?
4 Geithner's predecessor at Treasury
5 "Bird" with a flexible nose
6 "Crimes and Misdemeanors" actor, 1989
7 Gâteau des ___ (Mardi Gras dessert)
8 Kicks in
9 Spawn
10 Mythological thread-cutter
11 Shower holder
12 Sacrilegious types
13 Freelance output: Abbr.
16 Red Rock State Park location
20 Spanish man's name that means "peaceful"
22 Just get (by)
24 Can.'s Northwest ___
26 Bribed
27 George Sand title heroine
28 Some snowmobiles
30 Dear
31 Bellini opera set in the English Civil War
33 Short and disconnected: Abbr.
35 Punctilious type, slangily
38 February 4th, to some?
39 Accepted
41 Chick magnet?
42 Slip
46 Fetch
48 "Same here"
49 Birthstone for most Leos
50 Be a slowpoke
52 "I am," in Italy
53 They might break up a plot
54 Turning point?
56 "Also, I almost forgot . . .": Abbr.
57 Doo-wop syllable

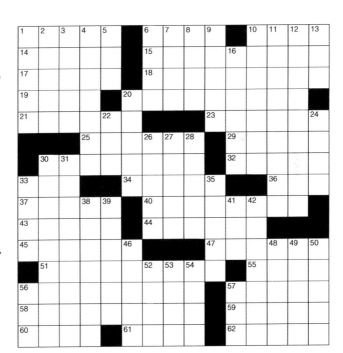

by Robin Schulman and Byron Walden

44

ACROSS

1 45, e.g.
5 Founding member of Public Enemy known for wearing large clocks around his neck
15 "___ at Duke's Place" (1965 jazz album)
16 2007 satirical best seller subtitled "And So Can You!"
17 ___ de Caña (Nicaraguan rum)
18 First British group since the Beatles to have two albums in the U.S. top 10 at the same time
19 "That's a great price!"
21 Strained
22 ___ sauce (sugary purée)
23 Run for it
25 Bygone medical ventilator
28 Hikes
32 Perfectly
33 Bldgs. with community courts
35 Building support
36 Area worth the most bonus troops in the game Risk
38 Literary captain who says "It's better to sail with a moody good captain than a laughing bad one"
40 About
41 Solid
43 More solid
45 Defunct ministry initials
46 Hatted bell ringers
48 "Relaciones Espirituales" writer
50 Fish also called a Jerusalem haddock
52 Site of a noted ancient league
53 Caustic soda, symbolically
56 One may cause your dinner to be spoiled
59 Out of it
61 Wet bar, maybe
63 2009 Lady Gaga hit
64 Oread in love with her own voice
65 One of an evil fairy tale duo
66 Three-player game

DOWN

1 "Fo' sho"
2 Distresses
3 What some plays are shown in
4 List quickly?
5 Alternative to a shake
6 Bachelor party entertainment
7 Date in France?
8 Spanish cows
9 Breakfast dish
10 Pump abbr.
11 9-Down variety
12 Money in the banca, once
13 Org. since 1920 with many staff lawyers
14 Sweeping
20 "For Better or for Worse" matriarch
24 "___ sine scientia nihil est" (Latin motto)
25 "Not for me"
26 Certain Afrocentrist
27 Bashes
29 Board game grande dame
30 Attempts to sink
31 Lady Liberty garb
34 Topic in artificial intelligence
37 Variety of zither
39 Age
42 Minor hit
44 Brand in contact lens care
47 Makings of a hero?
49 Some salon jobs
51 Papa Bear of Chicago football
53 Bills
54 Gut course?: Abbr.
55 Adjective for a coach house inn, maybe
57 "___ pis!" ("Too bad!," in France)
58 Nelson's catchphrase on "The Simpsons"
60 ___ Banos, Calif.
62 Where the chips fall where they may?

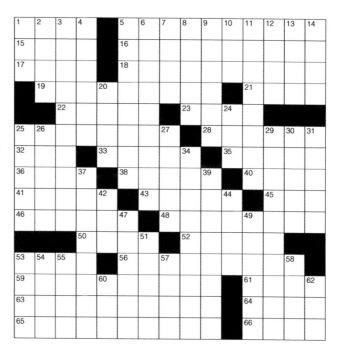

by Natan Last

ACROSS

1 Frame job
6 Taste
11 Somme summer
14 Love to pieces
15 Clara Barton, e.g.
16 Rank above maj.
17 Michelle Obama and Laura Bush
19 Singer Yoko
20 Sicilian spewer
21 On a grand scale
22 Somersault
23 Highway troopers
26 Of greatest age
29 Poi source
30 The Beach Boys' "___ John B"
31 Drinker's next-day woe
35 Submarine sandwich
36 Early synthesizers
38 Great review
39 Eave
41 Tendon
42 Cubes in a casino
43 E-mail predecessor
45 Oppressive regime
49 ___ Canal, waterway through Schenectady
50 "___ la Douce"
51 Lane of the Daily Planet
55 Beachgoer's shade
56 Tenet of chivalry
59 Had something
60 Assists at a heist
61 Cosmetician Lauder
62 Plural of "la" and "le"
63 West Pointer
64 Unexpected win

DOWN

1 Opposite of "out" in baseball
2 Tighten the writin'?
3 Ripped
4 ___ Major
5 Hamster, for one
6 Speak sharply to
7 Bad news for a taxpayer
8 Sticker
9 Sugar suffix
10 Hi-___ monitor
11 Food-poisoning bacteria
12 Gin's partner
13 Run off to a judge in Vegas, say
18 Allows
22 Put the pedal to the metal
23 Mo. when fall starts
24 Lousy reviews
25 U.R.L. ending that's not "com" or "gov"
26 Mt. McKinley's is 20,320 ft.
27 Oral history
28 Like a dire situation
30 HBO rival
31 Animal in a sty
32 It shows which way the wind blows
33 At any time
34 FF's opposite
36 Spray used on rioters
37 Completely biased
40 Drunk's outburst
41 Jeanne d'Arc, e.g.: Abbr.
43 Least plausible, as an excuse
44 Hellenic H's
45 Daisy part
46 Pontificate
47 Actors speak them
48 Hackneyed
51 Daffy Duck has one
52 Table scraps
53 "Now you're making sense"
54 Proofreader's "reinstate" mark
56 Fond du ___, Wis.
57 Atty.'s org.
58 Fire: Fr.

by Adam G. Perl

ACROSS

1 It began commercial service in '76
4 Chinese dynasty at the time of Christ
7 Cartoon featured in 23 best-selling books
14 1983 Randy Newman song
16 Brazier
17 Thingamajigs
18 Partly paid back
19 -
21 Fair-hiring inits.
22 Silverstein who wrote "The Giving Tree"
23 Backbreaking
27 Mattress brand
30 In America
34 Splinter group
37 Quaker product
38 "Star Wars" surname
39 Like "be": Abbr.
40 Figure that shares a property with this puzzle
42 Mercury or Saturn
43 Harmonic singing style
45 Member of the Be Sharps on "The Simpsons"
46 Equestrian's grip, maybe
47 -
48 Page of music
50 Michelin Man makeup
52 "___ Anything" ("Oliver!" song)
55 Reggae relative
58 Where marmots and chamois live
62 Hearten
66 Composer Antonio
67 Nixon policy
68 Came out
69 -
70 ___ Peres (St. Louis suburb)
71 Work of Alexander Pope

DOWN

1 Outdoor retail promotion
2 Oodles
3 Feldshuh of "Brewster's Millions"
4 Disturb a stand-up routine
5 Malt beverages
6 Nimbus launcher of 1964
7 Number that looks like the letter yogh
8 Step on it
9 Withdraw
10 Carrier overseer, for short
11 "Roméo et Juliette" section
12 Stat starter
13 -
15 Most repellent
20 Type of terrier
24 Express romantic interest in
25 Powerful kind of engine
26 "___ Can Cook" (former cooking show)
28 Critic who's a real thumb-body?
29 Quick expression of gratitude
31 Caesar dressing?
32 Like ink, poetically
33 -
34 Graze, in a way
35 Olympic archer
36 Be exultant
40 Uto-Aztecan language
41 Valedictorian's pride: Abbr.
44 Punster
46 Above the ground
49 Lord and lady
51 Foreign dignitary
53 Muralist Rivera
54 One way to turn right
55 Southwestern rattler
56 Had down
57 Palio di ___ (Italian horse race)
59 Like some clothing
60 "The ___ Game" (1965 Shirley Ellis hit)
61 -
63 Put down, in a way
64 Colts, on a scoreboard
65 Rural env. abbr.

by Patrick Blindauer

ACROSS

1 Office device appropriate for this puzzle?
7 Await
11 Rte. suggester
14 Setting for many a fairy tale
15 Assistant played by Charles Bronson in "House of Wax"
16 Drama set in Las Vegas
17 Command agreement
18 "That's of little importance"
20 Out of service?: Abbr.
21 Road hazards
23 Fence builder's starting point
24 Small doses may come in them
26 "Charlotte's Web" girl
27 One half of an old comedy duo
28 Like the Paris Opera
31 Airport need
34 Substitute
37 I.R.S. 1040 line item
38 They might give each French kisses
39 Way to get around something
40 No longer interested in
41 Undecided: Abbr.
42 Album half
43 Space under a desk
44 End of a perfect Sunday drive?
46 Grill
48 Impulse path
49 33-Down's group, with "the"
53 Kitchen tool
55 Physicist Bohr
56 Jim Beam product
57 Like some patches
59 1940s British P.M.
61 Times in classifieds
62 Game played on a world map
63 Quick outing for Tiger Woods . . . or what this completed puzzle contains
64 Violin cutouts
65 What a peeper uses to peep
66 Can't stand

DOWN

1 Game item usually seen upside-down
2 Check writer
3 Is of ___ (helps)
4 Some Windows systems
5 The Cutty Sark, for one
6 Lifesavers, say
7 Features of homemade cameras
8 Big ones can impede progress
9 Montréal or Québec
10 Window dressing
11 Feigns ignorance
12 Play ___ (perform some songs)
13 Seal's opening?
19 Conflicted
22 Photography aid
25 Portable info-storing devices
26 Below-ground sanctuary
29 Almond or pecan
30 Batting helmet feature
31 Filthy place
32 Prefix with valent
33 See 49-Across
35 Pre-schoolers?
36 Light-blocking
39 Part of a home security system?
40 French eleven
42 Ones who sleep soundly?
43 Alley behind a bar on TV?
45 They're drafted for service
47 Higher ground
49 Topographical feature formed by underground erosion
50 1957 hit for the Bobbettes
51 Parts of masks
52 "Thou ___ I have more flesh than another man": Falstaff
53 Role for which Marion Cotillard won a 2007 Best Actress Oscar
54 Vest feature
55 Like a quidnunc
58 Feature of many a ballroom dance
60 "We Know Drama" channel

by Mike Nothnagel

48

ACROSS

1 ___ hole
7 Early film star who wore lipstick in the shape of a heart
15 Severe sales restriction, informally
16 Plunge
17 City that's home to Parliament Hill
18 Has a service break?
19 Reqmt. for giving someone the third degree?
20 Some compact light sources
22 Try to fit a square peg in a round hole, e.g.
23 With 8-Down, takes a lot of shots, say
24 Non-union?
25 Suggest for the future
26 ___ B (first step)
27 Sweltered
28 ___ Farm, setting for a George Orwell story
29 Member of a campaign staff
31 National Wear Red Day mo.
32 Came out of a hole, say
33 Continues, as a band
37 Its first two vols. covered 43-Across
38 Top-level commands, collectively
39 Hard to discern
42 Pin in a hole
43 See 37-Across
44 "Dinner's ___ "
45 Measures of volume
46 House of prayer
47 Spirited response?
48 Runs up
49 Farm shelter
50 "Uh-huh"
52 Iberian city that lends its name to a variety of wine
54 It's not useful in a long shot situation
55 Food writer Nigella
56 Extremely touching?
57 Noted TV twins

DOWN

1 "You played well"
2 Maryland's historic ___ Creek
3 Litter pickup place?
4 South's declaration, perhaps
5 Mint
6 Like rulers
7 Toronto landmark
8 See 23-Across
9 Solicited
10 Actor Roger
11 Things that pop up annoyingly
12 Crunch
13 Go too far
14 One in an outfit
21 Approved, as a contract
25 Subject of a 1980s surrogacy case
27 Produce
28 Not accidental
30 Coin with a hole in it
31 Goes it alone
33 Worker with street smarts?
34 Fish whose male carries the eggs
35 Starting point?
36 Bundles of bound quarks
38 Something from which something else is taken away
39 As an example
40 "Star Wars" name
41 Brew
42 "Way to be, man!"
45 [Bo-o-o-oring!]
46 Junk vehicles
48 Peculiar: Prefix
51 In addition
53 Bud

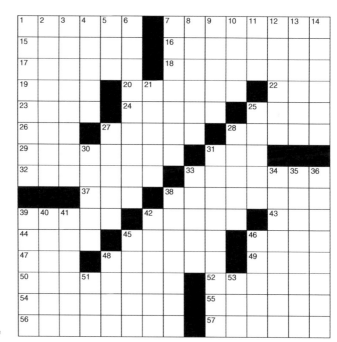

by Mike Nothnagel

ACROSS

1 "Caro nome," for one
5 Gov. Faubus in Arkansas history
10 Black
14 Bryn ___
15 Unsuspecting
16 Second to ___
17 *"I don't know yet"
20 Comment put in by Putin, perhaps
21 Ballet headliners
22 Decide to take, with "for"
24 *1968 #2 hit heard in "Easy Rider"
27 Grp. at home on the range?
28 To ___ (just so)
29 English fashionista Bartley
33 Air or ami preceder
34 Biblical verb with "thou"
36 Aligns
37 "Yo te ___"
38 Ill-fated . . . or a hint for answering the six starred clues
40 Hit Jerry Bruckheimer TV drama
41 Scorch
43 Boozer
44 Sportage maker
45 Applies
47 They may be boxed
49 Over there
50 *1924 Isham Jones/ Gus Kahn song
52 Interview part: Abbr.
53 Hollywood's Anderson and Reed
56 Diamond on a record player
58 *"No WAY!"
63 Character in "Beowulf"

64 Alternative to hash browns
65 Through
66 People mover since 1853
67 Vintner's need
68 What a rake may do

DOWN

1 Tsp. or tbsp.
2 When repeated, excited
3 *Memorable movie quote of 1932
4 Like many a gallerygoer
5 Length in years of a lenient sentence, maybe
6 Head of the Egyptian god Amun
7 Through

8 Arthur Miller play "___ From the Bridge"
9 Soup variety
10 Person with special access
11 Good name for someone born on Dec. 25
12 What might give a physical reaction?
13 Wishes
18 Old WB sitcom
19 Substance in a chemistry experiment
22 In a position to steal
23 Blend before using
25 Vaquero's rope
26 Snug, as in bed
30 *Like someone who's had a narrow escape
31 Wound
32 Chinese, e.g.

35 Sweet wine of Hungary
38 Irk
39 Certain English poetry scholar
42 Feels a loss
46 Hirsute
48 Took to court
51 "That's ___ subject"
53 Fire starter?
54 Follower of juillet
55 San Francisco's public transit system, with "the"
57 Favorite
59 ___ Maria
60 Pawn jumpers: Abbr.
61 Formerly
62 [Mumble, mumble]

by Charles Deber

ACROSS

1 "Come to ___"
5 Second-highest peak in the Cascades
11 Brown, for one
14 Big production
15 Lethargy
16 J.F.K. overseer
17 Lean and tough
18 Poke holes in
19 Army fig.
20 One who went to school in Middletown, Conn.
23 Blue part of a map
24 "Sure!"
25 WB show named for its star
28 Unite
29 It's stranded
32 First name in Communism
33 Actress Milano of "Charmed"
36 Kitchen supervisor, sometimes
37 Like the 1995 film "Sense and Sensibility"
40 Quarterback Phil
41 Dressed like Cinderella
42 "The Magic Flute" parts
43 Go on and on
44 Sei halved
47 ___ Station
48 Jennifer Lopez album "J to ___ LO!"
51 Whitish
53 It's based in Tripoli
57 Ruckus
59 Slight, in a way
60 Miles off
61 Remembrance Day mo.
62 Activity in which nothing is going on?
63 Drew (near)
64 Anger, with "off"
65 Hits the 5 and 10, say
66 Place for a pad

DOWN

1 Huddle
2 For one
3 Puckered
4 Refuges
5 Not leave home
6 Many a gardener
7 Set forth
8 Garden tool
9 Add
10 Province
11 In case it's called for
12 Hoover, e.g., informally
13 N.B.A.'s ___ Ming
21 Like a Möbius strip
22 Timed sporting events
26 Spanish newborn
27 Tatyana of "Fresh Prince of Bel Air"
30 Big Apple inits.
31 ___ Spumante
32 Its home is on the range
33 Stylish suit
34 D.C. V.I.P.
35 "Not ___ eye . . ."
37 Desperate
38 Romantic Sammy Cahn/Jule Styne song
39 Sheep's cry
40 Easy mark
44 1981 thriller about a stalker
45 Call again?
46 Big part of an order
48 Binding
49 Odyssey or Passport
50 To have, in Paris
52 Kiss
54 Trash sites
55 Language of the British Isles
56 Radiation units
57 Fire ___
58 Forest female

by David Liben-Nowell and Ryan O'Donnell

ACROSS

1 Slightly sharp or flat, as a voice
7 Insects in swarms
14 Encroachment
15 Retired Big Apple basketball player?
16 What tests test
17 Expounds upon
18 English racing site
19 "Das Rheingold" goddess
20 Brit's oath
21 Was well-versed in a will?
25 Sawbones
26 Hot time in la cité
27 Make in a cauldron
31 R-rated, maybe
34 Lock
38 Guinevere, to Lancelot?
41 Like some suspects
42 Lunch site
43 Kids' stuff
44 What you might get in a booth
46 Roxy Music co-founder
48 Macramé company's goal?
55 Cyclades island
56 Sorrows
57 Bloopers, e.g.
60 Miss the start, maybe
63 Theme song from "American Gigolo"
64 Select a sweater?
65 Even
66 Trigonometric ratios
67 Run in

DOWN

1 Torre Pendente city
2 Prepares, as the presses
3 What a king may win
4 List preceder
5 Stopped
6 Upholsterer's meas.
7 Oafs
8 Think up
9 Bank drafts: Abbr.
10 "Gimme ___!" (repeated cry of a University of Mississippi cheerleader)
11 Griminess
12 Follow, as advice
13 Woman's golf wear
15 Meanie
19 Blah, blah, blah
22 Woman-chaser
23 Ltr. routing aid
24 Earn
27 ___-ray Disc
28 Dorm heads, for short
29 E-mail address ending
30 Jane of "Father Knows Best"
32 "Huh?"
33 Puts off
35 Kind of boost
36 Short
37 Many figs. on stained-glass windows
39 Norwegian king
40 Numbers game
45 "Uh, hold on! That's wrong!"
47 Like things said after cutting to a commercial
48 Fun
49 "___ Is to Blame" (1986 hit)
50 Of element #76
51 University mil. programs
52 Look through half-closed blinds, e.g.
53 Less healthy
54 Type squiggle
58 Aussie runners
59 Number of dwarfs with Blanche Neige
61 Theta preceder
62 Hosp. staffer
63 Windy City transportation org.

by Mike Torch

52

ACROSS

1. It may be hand-picked
6. Not express
11. "The word"
14. Deep blue
15. Earthy tone
16. Brian who produced or co-produced seven U2 albums
17. Feeling of nonfulfillment
19. "Wait Wait . . . Don't Tell Me!" network
20. Went for, at an auction
21. Playing marbles
23. Case of bad spelling?
24. Frequent home acquisition
26. Fill in for
29. Big __
30. Friend of Falstaff
31. Szyslak of Springfield
32. "Come on, pack your stuff . . . !"
35. Signs
38. Statement about 17-, 24-, 49- and 59-Across
41. "Baseball Tonight" network
42. Hall-of-Fame QB/kicker George
43. With 45-Down, "Trust No One" series
44. Fandango offerings, slangily
46. "__ Dalloway"
47. Arterial implant
49. Burgers and fries, often
52. Orch. section
53. Aggrieved person's cry, maybe
54. Bill & __ Gates Foundation
58. "My Big Fat Greek Wedding" actress Vardalos

59. Item that may have a date stamp
62. Comprehended
63. Like 36 piano keys
64. Original Thanksgiving fare
65. Cosine of 2 pi
66. Where Moses received the Law
67. Kingly title in Spanish

DOWN

1. Big Broadway hit
2. It might be a lot
3. Neither masc. nor fem.
4. Violinist Heifetz
5. Surreptitiously
6. Whites or darks, say
7. Mo. of Indigenous Peoples Day
8. Christogram part
9. Bellowing
10. Extent
11. Internal memo?
12. Let off the hook?
13. Robert who won a Tony for "How to Succeed in Business Without Really Trying"
18. Kingly title in Latin
22. Another time
24. Colonel suspected of murder
25. Hearts, e.g.
26. French girlfriend
27. Barracks lineup
28. Maybe takes one risk too many
29. Sailor's patron
33. Recede
34. Rubber-stamped
36. Former baseball commissioner Bowie
37. "Leave it in" mark
39. "Clear Light of Day" author Desai

40. Town near New London, Conn.
45. See 43-Across
48. Like "Survivor" councils
49. Bat used for fielding practice
50. Chloride or carbonate
51. Graceful African antelope
52. Homily: Abbr.
54. Polite request for permission
55. Hard-boiled, in a way
56. Nod off
57. "The House Without __" (first Charlie Chan mystery)
60. __ mot
61. Uracil-containing macromolecule

by Joon Pahk

ACROSS

1 *Start of a 38-Across
5 "The Good Earth" heroine
9 So last year
14 ___ about
15 *Small part of a spork
16 Recyclable item
17 Prayer wheel user
18 *Musical quality
19 Strike down
20 Cockpit announcements, briefly
21 Millstone
22 *Made tracks
23 Strength
25 Cord unit
27 Good name for an investment adviser?
29 Permanently attached, in zoology
32 Early MP3-sharing Web site
35 *Teed off
37 Up-to-date
38 Hint to the word ladder in the answers to the starred clues
43 ". . . and that's final!"
44 *Put into piles
45 Canal site, maybe
47 Showing irritation
52 Last in a series
53 Toxic pollutant, for short
55 Sweet, in Italy
56 *Locale in a western
59 Many Christmas ornaments
62 Holly
63 Crossword maker or editor, at times
64 *It may precede a stroke
65 Rat Pack nickname

66 Dirección sailed by Columbus
67 *Ax
68 Change components, often
69 Dag Hammarskjöld, for one
70 Some cameras, for short
71 *End of a 38-Across

DOWN

1 At minimum
2 How baseball games rarely end
3 Kind of land
4 Undoes
5 Camp Swampy dog
6 Symbol of courage
7 Undo
8 "Kinsey" star, 2004
9 Orkin victim
10 Survivalist's stockpile
11 Full of energy
12 "The Way of Perfection" writer
13 Word after red or dead
24 Solomon's asset
26 In profusion
28 Pseudo-cultured
30 Stockpile
31 Muff one
33 Like some men's hair
34 Nasdaq buy: Abbr.
36 Wynn and Harris
38 Quick drive
39 Tried out at an Air Force base
40 Theater for niche audiences
41 Medical research org.
42 Doo-___
46 Shows scorn
48 Lacking
49 "Fighting" athletes
50 Part of an act, perhaps
51 Simple sugar
54 Range setting
57 On Soc. Sec., say
58 Trap, in a way
60 Winter exclamation
61 Goes with
63 Orgs. With "Inc." in their names

by Barry C. Silk

54

ACROSS
1 Parroting sorts
6 Stud on a stud farm
10 Good name, casually
13 Venue for some clowns
14 Word before city or child
15 Basis for some discrimination
16 Mystery desserts?
18 Thing to roll over, in brief
19 East ___, U.N. member since 2002
20 Central part
22 Oscar winner Sorvino
25 Acquired relative
27 Musical with the song "Mr. Mistoffelees"
28 Equal to, with "with"
30 O.K. to do
32 Orange feature
33 Bates's business, in film
35 Video shooter, for short
38 Direction from K.C. to Detroit
39 Stir up
41 ___-Ida (Tater Tots maker)
42 Top end of a scale
43 Miming dances
44 Visibly frightened
46 Bucky Beaver's toothpaste
48 High-hats
49 Soprano Gluck
51 Refrain syllables
54 "Spare me!," e.g.
55 Place for a lark
57 Winter coat feature
59 Diamond corner
60 Sculler's affliction?
65 Time of anticipation
66 First-rate
67 Many an art film

68 ___ judicata
69 Hebrides isle
70 Take as one's own

DOWN
1 Flight board abbr.
2 Samoan staple
3 Byrnes of TV's "77 Sunset Strip"
4 Reason for a long delay in getting approval, maybe
5 Arias, e.g.
6 Motorist's headache
7 Calligrapher's buy
8 Period of seven days without bathing?
9 Gaelic tongue
10 What the sky might do in an inebriate's dream?
11 Everglades denizen
12 Belfry sounds

14 Pic to click
17 Mideast V.I.P.
21 Zenith competitor
22 "Impression, Sunrise" painter
23 Cockamamie
24 Illustrations for a Poe poem?
26 Choir voices
29 Leader of the pack
31 Pick up bit by bit
33 Place for a crown
34 In vitro items
36 Mountain ridge
37 Group with a meeting of the minds?
40 Employment in Munchkinland?
45 Choir voice
47 Inflate, in a way
48 Spilled the beans
49 Honey-hued

50 Take a powder
52 Sitcom with the catchphrase "Kiss my grits!"
53 ___ sausage
56 Tolkien beasts
58 "Beowulf," e.g.
61 Modus operandi
62 Courtroom vow
63 Barely beat
64 The "all" in "Collect them all!"

by Robert A. Doll

55

ACROSS

1 Electrical bridges
5 Disney output, once
9 Winter warmer
14 Polo on TV
15 Place to pay a toll, perhaps
16 Jude Law title role
17 "___ unrelated note . . ."
18 Buggy place?
19 4×100 meters need
20 Genghis Khan's non-pedigree domain?
23 George ___, longest-reigning English king
24 Round fig.
25 Narrowest winning margin in baseball
28 Rush hour pace
30 Word after pen or gal
32 Newcastle's river
33 Be indisposed
35 In the thick of
37 So last year
38 Non-pedigree essential courses?
42 Monopolist's portion
43 Margin marking
44 Author of "The Island of the Day Before"
45 "___ Houston" of 1980s TV
47 Far from welcoming
48 You can open with them
52 Repugnant
54 Letters on tires
56 Talladega unit
57 Casey's non-pedigree team?
61 Put on the books
63 Trial balloon, e.g.
64 Dr. Pavlov
65 Bat maker's tool
66 Pundit Colmes
67 Be disposed (to)
68 Burgers on the hoof
69 For fear that
70 Bullpen stats

DOWN

1 Like superprecise clocks
2 "The Bathers" painter
3 Head cases?
4 Be a fink
5 Hands over
6 Jump for joy
7 Singles bar delivery
8 Pipe part
9 Salk contemporary
10 Bordeaux wine
11 Words from Alphonse or Gaston
12 Ipanema locale
13 Place for reeds
21 Items in some illicit trade
22 Miranda rights readers
26 "One" on a coin
27 Court divider
29 Cabinet department until 1947
30 Kegger, e.g.
31 "___ losing it?"
34 Elizabethan ballad player, maybe
36 Ernie the Muppet's rubber toy
38 Decked out
39 Frisbee game involving body contact
40 Nonacademic school activities, informally
41 Chaney of "The Wolf Man"
42 Latin 101 word
46 "You got me!"
49 Twist of fiction
50 Potassium source
51 Goes on a spree
53 Out-and-out
54 Results of some bargains
55 Apply spin to
58 Baby bottle?
59 On one's duff
60 Time on a marquee
61 Ways around Chi-town
62 N.L.'er since 2005

by Fred Piscop

ACROSS
1 "That's ___ . . ."
4 Moo ___ pork
7 You don't want it beaten out of you
10 A minimus is the smallest one
13 Ritz-___ hotels
15 Expert at interpreting a text
17 It's "ascending" in a Vaughan Williams piece
18 Contents of a lode
19 E'er
21 Justin Timberlake's former group
22 Badlands sight
23 "___ te llamas?" (Spanish 101 question)
26 Hammarskjöld of the U.N.
28 Inspiration for Hunter S. Thompson
31 Egg: Prefix
32 Heir
36 Dudes
37 Blow away
38 La mer, e.g.
39 Uncle of fiction
40 Eyre
43 "Winnie the Pooh and Tigger ___"
44 "Beetle Bailey" dog
45 Not budging
46 Talks one's head off
47 Instrument you blow into
50 Low-lying wetland
53 Air
58 Zagat's readers, informally
59 Ape
60 Cheese for French onion soup
61 It may be hidden under a shirt
62 "___ Mine" (1957 hit by the Platters)
63 Sault ___ Marie

64 Cincinnati-to-New York dir.
65 Pip at the start of "Great Expectations," e.g.

DOWN
1 Prefix with -gon
2 Actress Arlene
3 Chose, as lots
4 Holds back
5 Equine
6 Bad behavior
7 Sub at the office
8 "Lost time is never found again," e.g.
9 Actress Zellweger
10 Flowerpot material
11 Buckwheat's affirmative
12 Electric ___
14 Grassy plain
16 Subtly suggests

20 Elite Eight org.
23 Money-saving restaurant offer
24 Flagrant
25 Like a stereotypically bad professor
27 Man-eating shark
29 Bygone Apple laptop
30 Autos for test-driving
32 Hair lacking care
33 Be in the red
34 Fire
35 Orange or plum
41 Nonentity
42 Boxer Willard defeated by Jack Dempsey for the world heavyweight title
46 Isaac Bashevis Singer story "___ the Yeshiva Boy"
48 Off-Broadway awards

49 Critic Roger
51 Capital of Jordan
52 Singer Frankie
53 Peeved
54 "Gotcha"
55 Ace
56 Highest European volcano
57 One of two in a 47-Across
58 Alphabet trio

by Oliver Hill

ACROSS

1 Figure in "The Lion, the Witch and the Wardrobe"
5 Kind of cuisine in which onions, bell peppers and celery are the "holy trinity"
10 Fake
14 Hoodwink
15 Jim Croce's "___ Name"
16 Tremendous
17 Hughes poem with the line "They send me to eat in the kitchen"
18 Introductory course, often
19 Cy Young winner Hershiser
20 Kind of puzzle suggested by this crossword's theme
23 Cleopatra used it as a beauty lotion
24 King, in Portugal
25 Carnivorous fish
28 Terse letter opener
31 Sweater type
35 Bonkers
37 Way to find your way: Abbr.
39 French rejection
40 End of a popular saying related to this puzzle's theme
44 Former telecom giant
45 Big name in kitchen gadgets
46 One way to be caught
47 Ed of "Roots"
50 How some packages arrive
52 Mice can be found around them
53 Blue
55 "The Rubáiyát" poet
57 How to link the 12 letters in this puzzle with a single line to make a picture

64 Drug ___
65 Quibble
66 "Mon ___!"
67 German car
68 Oreo filling
69 Author Dinesen
70 Surveyor's map
71 Baseball pioneer Doubleday
72 Big lugs

DOWN

1 Bank protector, for short
2 Camera setting
3 Agreed ___
4 Just after birth
5 Internet equipment powerhouse
6 Semiprecious stones
7 Big bump
8 Logan's locale
9 Candidate trailing Bush and Gore
10 Sure thing
11 Banged up
12 A long, long time
13 Florida senator Martinez
21 "Maria ___," 1941 #1 hit
22 The "D" in R&D: Abbr.
25 "___ song of sixpence"
26 Sheepshanks, e.g.
27 John Denver wrote two songs about this town
29 Abode north of the Arctic Circle
30 Univ. in Troy, N.Y.
32 ___ Gay
33 Doer of stand-up
34 Gardeners may work on them
36 Prefix with tourism

38 What one might do in 27-Down
41 A+: Abbr.
42 1940s computer
43 Equipment with a headset
48 Sparkle and wit
49 College cheer
51 Sit behind bars
54 Bangladesh's capital, old-style
56 Athlete who's not dashing?
57 Blue, south of the border
58 Russian car
59 Unnice comment
60 Balanced
61 Precursor of the Apple Macintosh
62 Dining table expander
63 Cheap laughs
64 Toy gun ammo

by Barry Boone

58

ACROSS
1 Gathering clouds, e.g.
5 Smooth-talking
9 Some N.C.O.'s
14 Centers of attention
15 Rock's partner
16 Sierra ___
17 Unencumbered
19 Shop group
20 Some fruit still lifes?
22 Parka wearer, maybe
25 Orbital extreme
26 Showy dance intro?
30 Security concerns
31 Diva's asset
32 Where one might get steamed
35 Suffix with buoy
36 Chocolate-caramel candies
37 In short order
38 Terse reproof
39 Actor Rutger ___
40 Political philosopher John
41 Gobbler in a powwow musical group?
43 Comical Boosler
46 Call for more
47 Chocolate's journey?
51 Prickly plant
52 Stateside
56 Where élèves study
57 Hosiery shade
58 "Hairspray" mom
59 Writer who went to hell?
60 Get blubbery
61 Novelist Jaffe

DOWN
1 Not quite oneself
2 Jersey sound
3 System starter?
4 Sweating the small stuff
5 Gradually appeal to
6 In the ___
7 Rick's film love
8 Totally bungled
9 7-Eleven cooler
10 Like half of U.S. senators
11 In action
12 It takes up to 10 yrs. to reach maturity
13 Pick up on
18 Priests of the East
21 Hunger signals
22 Super success
23 Composer Camille Saint-___
24 Natural ability
27 "Are you in ___?"
28 Archaeologist's prefix
29 Huge, in verse
32 Super, in Variety
33 Cincinnati and lowball are versions of this
34 In the blink of ___
36 Japanese bowlful
37 Dungeons & Dragons character
39 Roasted one
40 Fencing move
41 Capulet murdered by Romeo
42 Get together for a task
43 Fell back
44 Poet Federico García ___
45 Negative particle
48 Penthouse asset
49 It's enough, for some
50 Easy to maneuver, at sea
53 Oath affirmation
54 "The Situation Room" airer
55 Rte. suggester

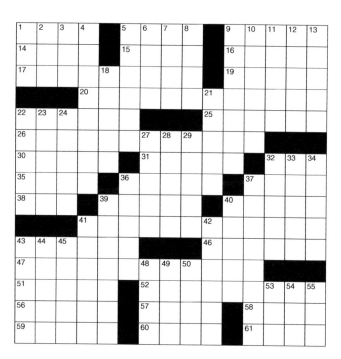

by Donna Hoke Kahwaty

The eight two-letter answers in this puzzle are all state postal abbreviations, representing (in some order) the Beaver State, Beehive State, Big Sky Country, Heart of Dixie, Pine Tree State, Show Me State, Sunflower State and Volunteer State.

ACROSS

1 1889 Jerome K. Jerome comedy novel
16 Undesirable alternatives
17 Bear, in old Rome
18 Some feds
19 Bill
20 See note
21 Office rewards
23 Carlo who married Sophia Loren
24 Anne who married Henry VIII
26 Not guzzle
27 See note
28 New Orleans-to-Indianapolis dir.
29 Put into office: Var.
33 Gas pump abbr.
34 Cry interrupting a prank
35 Bank book entry
36 Schubert's "The ___ King"
37 Comparative suffix
38 Like a certain route
39 "You mean me?"
40 Telecom setup
41 More, it's sometimes said
43 Langley, e.g.: Abbr.
44 Yearbook div.
45 Indulge
46 Something with this is not neat
47 See note
48 Game piece in Hasbro's The Game of Life
49 One who knows what's suitable?
51 Alternative to "take out"
53 Young haddocks
56 See note
57 Jefferson bills
58 Classic TV role for Ronny Howard

59 Beautiful woman of paradise
61 Dessert not for the calorie-conscious
64 Some awards for accomplishment

DOWN

1 Outline
2 Whence the line "A person's a person, no matter how small"
3 Purview of the I.C.C.
4 Accustom (to)
5 Made an effort
6 See note
7 Certain newts
8 Finger
9 Time of danger
10 "Delta of Venus" author
11 See note
12 Swing alternative

13 Warning sign
14 Something customary
15 Pushing beyond proper limits
22 Superior canal locale
23 Painter Mondrian
25 Overhears, perhaps
26 Heel style
30 Short burst
31 Joe who was twice A.L. Manager of the Year
32 Light ___
33 Forward
41 Footwear giant Thom ___
42 One who won't move over
48 1973 War hit "The ___ Kid"
50 "God ___ refuge" (start of Psalm 46)
52 Pixar drawing

53 Not really fight
54 Part of a mileage rating
55 Shoot in a swamp
58 Pay extender?
60 Service
62 See note
63 See note

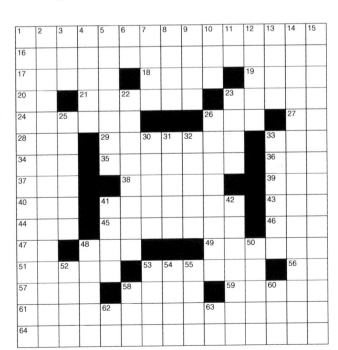

by Joe Krozel

ACROSS

1 Centrally located
6 Ambitious in scope
10 Reaction to poison oak
14 Vacant, in a way
15 Black-tie affair
16 Red Muppet
17 Tricky, unexpected questions
19 Mid sixth-century year
20 It's a relief
21 Spies seek them
23 Experiment site
24 Vampire's undoing
25 Pirate's storage
28 Super deal
29 "Hurlyburly" Tony winner Judith
30 Web address
31 Summer Games org.
32 Letters on some churches
33 What 17-, 24-, 48- and 57-Across are
40 Prefix with -asian
41 "Man's the ___, and Wealth the vine, / Stanch and strong the tendrils twine": Emerson
42 Place to refuel
43 Doctor of ___ (degree)
45 Subj. for aliens
46 Winter Palace residents
48 Stairway hazards, in some homes
50 Meadow mother
51 Galena or anglesite
52 "Nice shot!"
56 Advantage
57 View from the shore
59 Reply to "That so?"
60 Unfeeling
61 Alamogordo trial
62 Dinette spot
63 Numbered work
64 Meddlesome sort

DOWN

1 Pay stub abbr.
2 Cross to bear
3 Grouse
4 12-Down hardware
5 Ogle
6 New York cardinal
7 Chum
8 "You bet!"
9 "Mighty" one who struck out
10 1948 John Wayne western
11 Make as a claim
12 Place with a forge
13 Use a block and tackle on
18 Splatter catcher
22 Gain altitude
24 Title for Camilla
25 Drop from the team
26 Initials for Camilla
27 One of football's Manning brothers
28 Science fair creation, briefly
31 Acre's locale: Abbr.
32 Source of bread, for short
34 Bulletin-creating department
35 Hearty enjoyment
36 Every one
37 Org. monitoring 38-Down quality
38 See 37-Down
39 Measures of gold purity: Abbr.
43 Purposely misinformed
44 Slowly, on a score
45 Glass in a medicine cabinet
46 Involving give-and-take
47 Unruffled
48 Calvin of fashion
49 Maine college town
50 Long, long time
52 Chatters
53 Rack holder
54 Fit snugly
55 "Dónde ___ . . . ?"
58 Australian runner

by Billie Truitt

ACROSS

1 Omani's money
5 It circles Hades nine times
9 Pro Football Hall of Fame coach who once played for the New York Yankees
14 Spanish pronoun
15 Runoff site
16 Airport rental option
17 Rube's opposite
19 Circle lines
20 Lets out
21 New York's __ Building, tallest in the world in 1930
22 Agonizes (over)
23 Submarine base?
25 Want ad letters
26 Graduated
28 Figs. in sports reports
31 See 7-Down
33 "Paradise Lost," e.g.
34 "Upidstay" language
37 Girl's name that's a butterfly genus
38 First name in erotic writing
39 Tow truck tool
42 Two- or three-year-old, maybe
43 Product introduced by 7-Down in 1971
45 Photography abbr.
46 "__ Mistress," 1982 horror flick
47 One for the road
50 1974 hit by Mocedades
52 Dog from Japan
54 Check attachments
56 What may be paid when someone dies
59 Make __ with the devil
60 Extra shuteye
61 Bank manager?
62 Stud fee?

63 River to the English Channel
64 Push (oneself)
65 Wee, informally
66 Liz Taylor's husband before Fisher

DOWN

1 Disqualify in court
2 Enjoys a lot
3 Potsdam Conference attendee
4 Knocks to the ground
5 Short moments
6 Receipts
7 Legendary name in 31-Across
8 See 37-Down
9 Sarcastic laugh
10 Bank feature
11 Orchid variety
12 Gallic girlfriend
13 It may be "bon"

18 Cyclades isle
21 Reunion group
24 Phone greeting in Central America
26 Former fleet member
27 Cub's home, for short
29 One of the Jacksons
30 Word with brain or price
31 Dart
32 Some batteries
33 Canal near Rome
34 Gait
35 Privy to
36 "Ben-Hur" extra
37 With 8-Down, one who grew up on MTV, maybe
40 Discontinued Saturn
41 Some QB protectors
43 Whom Taylor defeated for president in 1848

44 Giant among Giants
46 Wedding band, maybe
47 "De Oratore" writer
48 Take care of
49 Scraped
51 Kitchen gizmo
52 Suitable
53 Lock opening
54 Prone to freckles
55 Ne plus ultra
57 Grub
58 Chop __
60 Actress __ Ling of "Sky Captain and the World of Tomorrow"

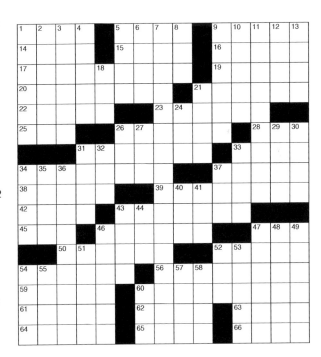

by David J. Kahn

62

ACROSS

1 Gave an order to
5 Fork
10 Woods call
14 Platinum Card offerer, for short
15 Shopping center
16 Shuffle or 67-Across, e.g.
17 Eliminate, with "out"
18 Symbol of thinness
19 Alternatives to creams
20 Arctic explorer post-fight?
23 Hatch or Byrd: Abbr.
24 Formerly, in high society
25 Possible cover for a siesta
27 Mood
29 Some offensive linemen: Abbr.
32 Off
33 "___ Love," 1975 Jackson 5 hit
35 "THAT guy!"
37 Past
38 Bows and arrows for Midas?
43 Was on the ticket
44 Major Indonesian export
45 Big inits. in Hollywood
46 1985 John Malkovich drama
49 Beseech
51 Convinced
54 Choice poultry
56 Use (up), as savings
58 Common suffix on chemical elements
60 Storage area for ribbed fabric?
64 Ladies' man
65 Inspector of crime fiction
66 Yearn (for)
67 See 16-Across
68 Model
69 Horse-drawn carriage
70 Switch possibilities
71 Level . . . or a three-word hint to 20-, 38- and 60-Across
72 Proctor's call

DOWN

1 Unpleasant remarks
2 Item worn around the neck, maybe
3 Presidential middle name
4 Prez, e.g.
5 Binge at the mall
6 Ladies' man
7 What many do on a day off
8 Polo alternative
9 Temporary covers
10 Singer of Rossini's "Largo al factotum"
11 Zero personality?
12 Pudgy
13 Money managers?: Abbr.
21 Massage
22 Night of poetry
26 Tight ___
28 Not even a little
30 Shakespearean title
31 English title
34 Big Apple cultural attraction, with "the"
36 Hosts
38 Enormous
39 Candy box size
40 Pen point
41 "___ mañana"
42 The "I" of Claudius I
43 Boombox button
47 Like some skiing
48 Not the party type?: Abbr.
50 Yellowstone Park attraction
52 Chinese fruit tree
53 Duke's home
55 Water pits
57 Copycatting
59 "The hell you say!"
61 Source
62 Roughly
63 Thomas with a pointed pen
64 Little, to Robert Burns

by Ari Halpern

ACROSS

1 Poor dating prospects
5 Central Africa's Lake ___
9 Place for a motto
14 M.P.'s quarry
15 Bloody, so to speak
16 Early British automaker Henry
17 Hot strip?
18 Washington has some big ones
19 Mountaineering equipment
20 Historical 1976 miniseries
23 $C_7H_5N_3O_6$
24 Toy at the beach
25 Close, old-style
27 Record holder
30 Refrigerator part
32 Big name in Gotham City
33 "Mens sana in corpora ___"
34 California's ___ Music Festival, since 1947
36 Goon
37 Juliet, e.g., in Gounod's "Romeo and Juliet"
40 Chapel Hill sch.
41 Only player to be part of three World Cup-winning teams
43 Poland's second-largest city
44 Tear
46 Obeys
48 Didn't raise
49 ___ light: Var.
50 Lay person?
51 Reverence
53 Punny hint to answering 20-Across, 11-Down and 29-Down
58 Sends
60 Object of ridicule
61 After-lunch bite

62 Black tea
63 Stick on a dish
64 Scraggy
65 It may be rounded up in a roundup
66 European capital
67 "Do the Right Thing" pizzeria

DOWN

1 Part of a pound
2 Out
3 Siesta
4 Abate
5 Hatch
6 Global legal venue, with "The"
7 Yankee nickname starting in 2004
8 1940s–'50s film/TV star with two stars on the Hollywood Walk of Fame

9 Cause for using a hot line
10 Sinbad's avian attacker
11 Classic 1947 detective novel
12 Process, in a way, as documents
13 Transcript
21 Biographies
22 ___ Station
26 Delivery notation: Abbr.
27 Give and take
28 It's sometimes grabbed
29 Bygone political slogan
30 '06 Series winner
31 Eastern royal
33 Title TV character in Bikini Bottom
35 Put away

38 Liquid fat
39 Prefix with sclerosis
42 Night school class, for short
45 Soldiers' jobs
47 Come-on
48 Not punishing sufficiently
50 One of the "Brady Bunch" kids
51 Cold-blooded killers
52 Stimulate
54 Holiday season
55 Quarter
56 "Hud" Oscar winner
57 Ones with charges
59 Writer who wrote "I became insane, with long intervals of horrible sanity"

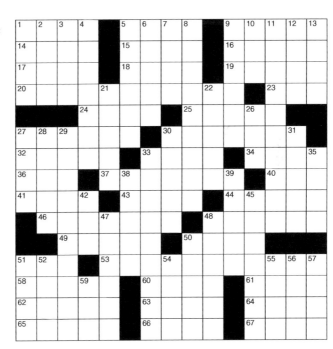

by Sheldon Benardo

TEEN PUZZLEMAKER WEEK

When this puzzle is done, connect the circled letters in alphabetical order, and then back to the start, to reveal something seen on the 32-Down 4-Down.

ACROSS
1 Waxed
5 First name in erotica
10 They might be chocolate
14 ___ Flynn Boyle of "Twin Peaks"
15 Request at a laundry
16 Like some keys
17 Dye plant
18 Popular women's fragrance
19 Together, in music
20 Makes people offers they can't refuse?
22 Apportionment
23 Set of values
24 View from Marseille
25 Relatives, slangily
27 You might end up with a bum one
30 Actress Tyler
31 Child, for one
34 Adler who outwitted Sherlock Holmes
36 ___ impulse
38 ___ + grenadine + maraschino cherry = Roy Rogers cocktail
39 Illumination of manuscripts, and others
40 Headline-making illness of 2002–03
41 Dis
42 Mushroom maker, for short
43 Tony nominee for "Glengarry Glen Ross"
44 Interrogator's discovery
45 Cultural org.
46 Retain
48 Rand who created Dagny Taggart
49 Striped quartz
53 ___ pop, music genre since the 1980s

55 Nocturnal bloodsucker
60 Tony Musante TV series
61 Extracted chemical
62 Punishment unit
63 Frost
64 Options during computer woes
65 James of jazz
66 Competitor of Ben & Jerry's
67 "Thus . . ."
68 Spotted

DOWN
1 Ruiner of many a photo
2 Charged
3 Filmmaker Von Stroheim
4 Theme of this puzzle
5 Without ___ (riskily)
6 It may be wrinkled
7 Ancient Semitic fertility goddess
8 Bakery employee
9 Elvis Presley's "___ Not You"
10 Detective's need
11 Like some six-packs
12 See 32-Down
13 Vile smile
21 That, to Tomás
26 Home of "The Last Supper"
27 Place for picnicking and dog-walking
28 Hill dwellers
29 ___ alla genovese (sauce)
30 City where 32- and 12-Down is found
31 Also sends to, as an e-mail
32 With 12-Down, locale of the 4-Down

33 "Ishtar" director
35 You might give a speech by this
37 Ultrasecret org.
47 "That mad game the world so loves to play," to Jonathan Swift
48 ___ ready
50 Peter out
51 It's often unaccounted for
52 Allen in American history
54 All ___
55 Lynn who sang "We'll Meet Again"
56 Port near the Red Sea
57 Yellow squirt?
58 Pie chart figs.
59 "Wishing won't make ___"

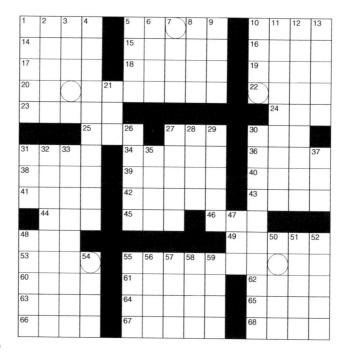

by Caleb Madison

ACROSS

1 Rock band with the triple-platinum album "High Voltage"
5 Direct sales giant
10 Ins. plan
13 Something sold in half sizes
14 Restraints
15 Orange Free State settler
16 Broken out, in a way
17 Liqueur flavoring
18 Constellation with a music-related name
19 Effects seen down the road
22 Be stingy with
25 Large container
26 Hollywood's Davis
27 ___ fat
28 Type on a computer
30 Peace of mind
31 Bed problem
32 Frame jobs
37 TV series that's now a film franchise
40 Chargers
41 Wall St. takeover
42 Faun, in part
43 Peak performance?
45 Call into question
46 Sought-after object
50 Big inits. in records
51 Popular Art Deco prints
52 Mischief-makers (you'll find seven of them in the answer grid)
55 Spear
56 Russian Literature Nobelist Ivan
57 Darned spot, often
61 Poetry ___
62 Follow, as a tip
63 Sauce maker
64 Scrabble 1-pointer

65 Offering a stark choice
66 Spontaneous skits

DOWN

1 Venom source
2 Curious George, for one
3 Can. Or Aust. money
4 Like some black tea
5 Open ___ of worms
6 Legume used to produce sprouts
7 Quills, sometimes
8 Out
9 Nieuwpoort's river
10 Big East basketball powerhouse
11 Polite Parisian's response
12 Deliver a stemwinder
15 Sights at many football games

20 Clip-___
21 Customs
22 Sap sites
23 Banded snake
24 Deadlock
29 Petro-Canada competitor
31 Passable
33 Seafood cocktail ingredient
34 Destroyer hunter
35 Almost win
36 Green and Rogen of comedies
38 Tennyson work
39 Nowhereness
44 Figure out
45 Drive forward
46 See for a second
47 Muscat money
48 Rockefeller Center figure
49 List unit

53 Web site with PowerSellers
54 ___ time
58 Plug's place
59 Immodesty
60 Verb on valentine candy

by Doug Peterson

ACROSS

1 Joshua's companion, in the Old Testament
6 Historic mansion in Newport, R.I., with "the"
10 Stone at a stream crossing
14 Done to death
15 Flood survivor
16 Former currency of Vatican City
17 Curl the hair of
18 Holey things
19 What some use to ply their craft?
20 Some Cubans in Texas?
23 Took a dip
24 Western end of I-190 near I-294
25 Where hot jazz developed?
31 Untighten
32 Untight
33 Have ___ at
36 "The emerald of Europe"
37 "Go, and catch a falling star" poet
38 Put one's foot down
39 Heartbreak
40 International Olympics chief Jacques
41 Up
42 Broadway deli offerings?
44 Japanese immigrant's child
47 Ends
48 20-, 25- and 42-Across, so to speak
54 Without ___ (unsafely)
55 How some quarterbacks go
56 Floated downstream, in a way
58 Wrapper weight
59 Start a hand, maybe
60 Greeting in an inbox
61 "Day Is Dying in the West," for one
62 Heath
63 Zero out

DOWN

1 Part of a price: Abbr.
2 Cunning
3 Ancient dynasty of northern China
4 Pre-Roman Roman
5 Affairs, slangily
6 Buggy field?
7 Wacko
8 Playwright Connelly
9 Division of Islam
10 They often go out on a limb
11 Piece among the crown jewels
12 Unwanted computer message
13 So last week
21 Follow (along)
22 Beverage brand whose logo is two lizards
25 Rowers
26 Purple Heart recipient
27 "Would ___?"
28 River below the Boyoma Falls
29 Silver topper?
30 Practice
33 Measurement with square units
34 Billy, e.g.
35 They may be even, ironically
37 Daily news quote, with "the"
38 Alcohol, slangily
40 Pull back (in)
41 Current measurer
42 Put in order
43 Black bag, maybe
44 Under, to a poet
45 "Uh-uh"
46 Kind of whale
49 Dis
50 Prefix with sphere
51 "I'm ___ you!"
52 Wharton degs.
53 Desiccated
57 Banned pesticide

by Ian Tullis

ACROSS

1 Part of a pay-as-you-go plan?
6 She'll "always have Paris"
10 Has obligations
14 Japanese brew
15 "Mighty" things
16 District in Hawaii
17 2008 Olympics tennis champion Dementieva
18 Meander, as a road
20 That over there
21 Author of "Something Wicked This Way Comes"
23 Inventor depicted in "The Prestige"
25 Long ago
26 Hinged apparatus
29 Walks down the aisle
31 Supplicate
33 Reverses course
37 Off-color
38 "Zounds!"
39 Like some calls left on answering machines
42 Diet
43 Leveler
45 Petrify
47 Cub raiser
50 M.P.'s concern
51 Music producer Brian
52 Walked off with
54 NATO member since 1982
57 Comparatively honest
59 Bopper
61 Crucial moment
64 1836 siege site, with "the"
66 Cadre, e.g.
67 "The Martha ___ Show" of 1950s TV

68 Scene of Hercules' first labor
69 Gang members
70 Comment about a loss
71 Upset

DOWN

1 Fully equipped and ready to go
2 Kitchen light
3 Emmy and Tony nominee Ryan
4 Blood
5 Equips
6 Tiny bit
7 "___ Miss Clawdy" (#1 R&B hit of 1952)
8 Winter vehicle
9 Guarantee
10 "Go ahead!"
11 Korean money
12 Doomsday, with "the"
13 Roman god of agriculture
19 Lock with no key?
22 Airport installation
24 Where the Riksdag meets
26 Kraft Foods brand
27 Be a cast member of
28 Cry from someone who's been aggrieved
30 Seek restitution, perhaps
32 Calif. barrio setting
33 Old country-and-western star ___ Travis
34 Over
35 Instrument unlikely to be heard at Carnegie Hall

36 1965 #1 hit by the Byrds
40 H
41 Search for water, in a way
44 Fix, as a pool cue
46 Aida, for one
48 Neighbor of Arizona
49 Tea, e.g.
53 Mount ___, second-highest peak in Africa
55 Part of Caesar's boast
56 Christener
57 Company leaders: Abbr.
58 G.P.S. output: Abbr.
60 Perfectly
61 Eventually appear
62 ___ bit
63 Zip
65 Book after Exod.

by Jim Hilger

68

ACROSS

1 Schmo
5 Trash cans and such
10 Walking encyclopedia
14 "How did ___ this happen?"
15 Opposite of someways
16 Alto lead-in?
17 Paris's ___ de Lyon
18 Benjamin
19 Wood alternative
20 Split
23 Refrain from singing in kindergarten?
24 Picketer's sign
28 Zing
29 Chinese dollar
33 All over
34 1990s war site
36 ___ feuilletée (puff pastry)
37 Primitive trophies . . . or a hint to this puzzle's theme
41 Karmann ___ (old Volkswagen)
42 Genuine
43 Alternative rock band with four platinum albums
46 Repair shop figs.
47 Cry out loud
50 Conformation defect in a horse
52 Words on a Wonderland cake
54 Traffic sign that indicates a possible temporary road closure
58 Deal preceder
61 Cause for pulling over
62 Where Samson defeated the Philistines
63 Lawless role
64 Managing, with "out"
65 Zest
66 Front
67 Go from one number to another
68 100 18-Acrosses

DOWN

1 Macrocephalic
2 Sainted king known as "the Fat"
3 Numbers in the thousands?
4 "S.N.L." alum
5 Creep
6 Gelato holder
7 "Pick me! I know the answer!"
8 Angry diner's decision
9 Egoist
10 Like a bishop's authority
11 Elongated fish
12 Day-___
13 One way to meet
21 "Happy birthday" follower
22 Back muscle, for short
25 Slightly
26 Fails to keep
27 It's barely passing
30 Seal's org.
31 "My Way" songwriter
32 Eleanor Roosevelt, to Teddy
34 Unable to think at all
35 Things with antennas
37 "Rich Man, Poor Man" novelist, 1970
38 Lie low
39 Wickiup, for one
40 Lightened
41 Test for M.A. seekers
44 Done, to Donne
45 Nut jobs
47 English essayist Richard
48 Certain Nebraska native
49 Lady Jane Grey's fate
51 ___-Mart
53 Shoelace tip
55 Ship part
56 Bausch & Lomb lens-care product
57 Playwright William
58 Chopping part of a chopper
59 French word in some bios
60 Former TV inits.

by Gary J. Whitehead

ACROSS

1 One of the Untouchables
5 Disney's "___ and the Detectives"
9 "That's great . . . not!"
14 Ryan of "Star Trek: Voyager"
15 Film character who says "Named must your fear be before banish it you can"
16 It's good for Juan
17 School ___
18 What might have the heading "Collectibles" or "Toys & Hobbies"?
20 Words with innocence or consent
22 Confused responses
23 Optimistic scan at the dentist's?
26 Not recorded
30 Boomer's kid
31 Org. in the Bourne series
32 Conjured up
34 Story of Ali Baba?
37 Many truckers
40 One may be caught in it
41 Sycophant
42 Transmits a message to Pancho and pals?
45 Pressing
46 Naut. heading
47 Letters on some churches
50 Scrabble 10-pointers
51 Amazes a horror film director?
55 Bond villain in "Moonraker"
56 Starters and more
57 Old street cry, or what's in 18-, 23-, 34-, 42- and 51-Across?

63 Bone meaning "elbow" in Latin
64 "Sorry, I did it"
65 A seeming eternity
66 Sale caveat
67 Conductor noted for wearing turtlenecks
68 Unfortunate date ending
69 Dickens's Mr. Pecksniff

DOWN

1 Marshalls competitor
2 Thin, overseas
3 Amount of debt, old-style
4 "I Am Spock" autobiographer
5 Socket filler
6 Kind of scene
7 Home of the City of Rocks National Reserve
8 Easy two points
9 They have bows
10 Ancient pillager
11 President Bartlet on "The West Wing"
12 "Wedding Album" recording artist
13 "That hurt!"
19 Prop on "The Price Is Right"
21 Pay strict attention to
24 Center of holiday decorations
25 Speak in Spanish
26 Racecar adornments
27 Furniture chain
28 Deal in
29 Swirl
33 Nay sayers
34 Essays
35 Second part of a three-part command
36 Dortmund denials

37 "Volver" actress, 2006
38 Not decent
39 Advantage
43 Unsetting look
44 Health supplement store
47 Tear off forcefully
48 Be serious
49 Long hyphen
52 Becomes fuller
53 Honor
54 Water colors
55 Precursor to Surrealism
57 Rock genre
58 Series finale
59 ?, on a sched.
60 Not even rare
61 Code carrier
62 "Poor venomous fool," to Shakespeare

by Kevin G. Der

ACROSS

1 Garland native to Minnesota
5 Not in the buff
9 With 46-Down, site of Cape Breton Island
13 English artist John who's buried at St. Paul's Cathedral
14 Potential sucker
15 The brother in "Am I my brother's keeper?"
16 Lawyers: Abbr.
17 Nickname for a dwarfish piano prodigy?
19 Sleeping cave denizen?
21 "First Blood" hero John
22 Musical sound before and after "da"
23 Comic Dunn and others
24 Bank
27 Collected
30 Adaptable truck, for short
31 Pickled pub quiz winner?
36 Musical Mitchell
38 Said with a sneer
39 Icicle site
40 Ships carrying a smelly gas?
43 Domingo, for one
44 Deli machine
45 One begins "By the rivers of Babylon, there we sat down"
47 Toast
49 Parenthesis, essentially
50 It may be organized
51 Comfy kids?
57 Pride of 12?
59 Bring (out)
60 Part of ABM

61 Move like molasses
62 Combative retort
63 ___ Verde National Park
64 1974 Sutherland/ Gould spoof
65 Contented sighs (and a homophonic hint to this puzzle's theme)

DOWN

1 Bruce Springsteen album "The Ghost of Tom ___"
2 ___ no good
3 Scatterbrain
4 Positive affirmation
5 Mobile home?
6 Counterpart of Apollo
7 Partially
8 Like 10-Down: Abbr.
9 Early Christian convert
10 Only president born in Hawaii
11 Shake, rattle and roll
12 High in the Sierra Madre?
17 "2001" studio
18 Maine university town
20 Unfeeling
23 Comparatively recent
24 1981 Stephen King novel
25 Complete
26 Ashcroft's predecessor
27 Like some waves
28 Online weekly, e.g.
29 Golf's ___ Cup
32 K. T. of country music
33 Early baby talk
34 Devilish

35 Chew (out)
37 People with this don't go out for very long
41 Actor Cary of "Twister"
42 Not at all stiff
46 See 9-Across
47 It can cure many things
48 Laugh-a-minute folks
49 Writer Rand
50 Chowder morsel
51 Prison, slangily
52 Black Sabbath singer, to fans
53 Pieces of pizza?
54 Celestial bear
55 Bite
56 Pontiacs of old
58 How many it takes to tango in Spain?

by Patrick Blindauer and Tony Orbach

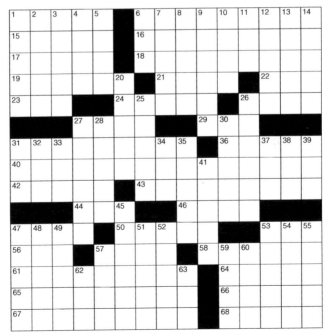

71

ACROSS

1 B-ball player
6 Like the Grand Canyon or Fourth of July fireworks
15 "Casablanca" co-star
16 Phobic sort
17 Prayer leaders
18 Rush job?
19 Broadway Joe
21 "American Pie" actress Tara
22 "Burma Looks Ahead" author
23 Head of steam?
24 Give __ (care)
26 Picasso's muse Dora __
27 De __ (by right)
29 Jocund
31 Cigar distributor, perhaps
36 Fictional hero on a quest to Mount Doom
40 Gets past a last difficulty . . . or a hint to this puzzle's theme
42 Creepy
43 Unisex
44 "Show pity, __ die": "The Taming of the Shrew"
46 Heading in a Keats volume
47 "Notch" on Orion's belt
50 Diaper, in Devon
53 Mandela's org.
56 Agcy. with agents
57 Stuff the piggy bank
58 Take, as an exam
61 Means of some W.W. I raids
64 Complete, quickly
65 Ousters
66 Crunching sound
67 Welcome January 1, say
68 1950s fad item

DOWN

1 New York City tour provider
2 Bodies of organisms
3 Suspended air travel?
4 Humorist Bombeck
5 Kick back
6 Hill denizen
7 __ smile (grin)
8 Calculus pioneer
9 Teeing off
10 Sud's opposite
11 Where you may get steamed
12 "The Taming of the Shrew" setting
13 1986 Turner autobiography
14 Showtime, at NASA
20 Strings pulled in heaven?
25 The end
26 Some aromatic resins
27 Sonny
28 Milk dispenser
30 Prior to, poetically
31 Paid intro?
32 Beluga delicacy
33 Joint possession word
34 __ Beta Kappa
35 Classical storyteller
37 Series opener
38 Part of many Dutch surnames
39 Hosp. areas
41 Buffalo Bill __ Wild West Show
45 Bad way to be caught
47 Teeny dress measurement
48 __ Fountain
49 Clinton's first defense secretary
51 Par __
52 Pasta variety
53 Run __ of
54 Bellini opera
55 Mysterious art visible from the sky
57 Green of "The Italian Job," 2003
59 Scratcher's target
60 Dolly Parton's "Travelin' __"
62 %: Abbr.
63 Milwaukee-to-Houston dir.

by Elizabeth C. Gorski

ACROSS

1 1970 hit for the Jackson 5
4 "Deal!"
10 What a loose thread might be
14 Friendly term of address
15 Rio crosser
16 Nest egg protectors
17 Name of Lord Rubble's feudal estate?
19 Slurs, in music
20 English princess
21 Sender of monthly checks: Abbr.
22 Fix, as a pump
24 Present addition
26 Air in a sooty shaft?
28 Removed roughly
32 Big Apple sch.
33 Sly little dog?
35 One stuck in the can
40 Third in a Latin series
41 Carefully search
43 Short evening?
44 Charles ___, "Brideshead Revisited" protagonist
46 Celebration for a Disney dwarf?
48 "The Mikado" wardrobe item
50 Like words?
51 Bamboozle a "Fargo" director?
56 Do sum work
57 Picasso/Braque movement
58 ___ Lingus
61 Title heroine described in the first sentence of her novel as "handsome, clever and rich"
64 It's shrinking in Asia
65 Property claim along the Rio Grande?
68 Realty ad abbr.
69 Alchemic knowledge

70 Mungojerrie or Skimbleshanks, in a musical
71 Wet septet
72 Toadies
73 P.G.A. Tour Rookie of the Year after Singh

DOWN

1 "Money, Money, Money" band
2 Muffin composition, maybe
3 Hot dog coating at a county fair
4 Mirror
5 "___ and Dolls"
6 Judges
7 Pioneer computer
8 Beach time in Bordeaux
9 Offset, as expenses
10 Gorge
11 Choisy-___ (Paris suburb)
12 Pawnbroker, in slang
13 Ruhr industrial hub
18 Recent arrival
23 Month before Tishri
25 Convex cooker
27 Betters
28 Romanov ruler
29 "___ Own" (song from "Les Miz")
30 DHL competitor
31 Sysop, for one
34 Place to overnight in an R.V.
36 Unbeliever
37 Meadow voles
38 Major conclusion?
39 Roger of "Cheers"
42 Sch. that's about 150 mi. north of 32-Across
45 Enormous birds of myth

47 Sumac from Peru
49 City visited in "Around the World in 80 Days"
51 Union foes
52 White-cap wearer
53 "The Audacity of Hope" author
54 Slumps
55 Pusher pursuers
59 Cheese choice
60 ___ Dubos, Pulitzer winner for "So Human an Animal"
62 Seder, e.g.
63 Creatures with tunnel vision?
66 Prospector's prize
67 Fled

by Patrick Blindauer

ACROSS

1 Examines a passage
6 Low islands
10 Some Morgan Stanley announcements, for short
14 Maker of Gauntlet and Area 51
15 Cousin of a heckelphone
16 Oscar winner Sorvino
17 Hospital employee's role as an opera girl?
19 Lord, e.g.
20 Swear words?
21 Mattress brand
22 Tiramisu topper
23 Locales for some orators
25 Attorney general before Reno
26 What Starkist decided to do for "Charlie"?
31 Circles overhead?
34 Carbonium and others
35 Boom preceder
36 Grace period?
37 Hard-to-refute evidence in court
39 Boarding zones: Abbr.
40 Veto
41 Does some floor work
42 In turmoil
43 A girl, born 8:48 a.m., weighing 6 pounds 13 ounces, e.g.?
47 You might be safe with them
48 Came out
52 Trajectories
54 Where some dye for a living
56 Band from Japan
57 Hollow response

58 Where a Hungarian toy inventor vacations in the Caribbean?
60 McAn of footwear
61 Valuable deposits
62 Goof-off
63 Orphan of literature
64 1976 top 10 hit for Kiss
65 Talk radio's G. Gordon ___

DOWN

1 Indian royalty
2 Exercise performed on a bench
3 Singer Neville
4 Vets, e.g.: Abbr.
5 Shop-closing occasions
6 Not cultured
7 Slightly
8 His planet of exile is Dagobah
9 Last word of "America the "America the Beautiful"
10 BMW, e.g.
11 Cobbler bottoms
12 Three-layer snack
13 Title sister played by Shirley MacLaine, 1970
18 ". . . bad as they ___"
22 Burmese and others
24 Not long from now
25 Most of the Ten Commandments, basically
27 A little stiff?
28 Furrow maker
29 Almost perfect?
30 Number two: Abbr.
31 Full house, e.g.
32 Gérard's girlfriend
33 Villain from DC
37 Pirouette points

38 Shower time: Abbr.
39 Train in a ring
41 Court stars, maybe, in brief
42 Knife, e.g.
44 Returnee's "hello!"
45 "Yum!"
46 Every which way
49 Creator of "Dick Tracy"
50 Fell back
51 Holder of secrets, often
52 Black ___, archnemesis of Mickey Mouse
53 Sore
54 "You betcha!"
55 Support when one shouldn't
58 Take the wrong way?
59 Year Saint Innocent I became pope

by Patrick Blindauer

74

ACROSS
1 Recreating
7 Commercial prefix with vision
10 Election night figs.
14 Ships whose rudders don't touch water
16 Sounds heard in a bowl
17 35-Across of 57-Across that equals 12-Down
18 Medical suffix
19 Bobsled challenges
20 Aesthete
22 The Big East's Panthers, for short
23 They travel through tubes
24 Winter driving hazards
26 Start of a Hemingway title
28 Less affluent
29 French novelist Robert ___, upon whose work the 1973 thriller "The Day of the Dolphin" is based
31 Philosopher Zeno of ___
32 Signature piece?
35 See 17- and 57-Across
38 Nav. rank
39 Container for folding scissors
41 Something a chair may hold
42 Pie crust pattern
45 Rubber gaskets
49 Endocrinological prefix
50 Status follower
51 Tolkien villains
53 Destination of Saul when he had his conversion, in the Bible

55 Reader of someone else's diary, say
56 Sparkling wine source
57 35-Across of 17-Across that equals 12-Down
59 Mideast's Gulf of ___
60 Neither high nor low
61 Half-dome construction
62 Govt. ID
63 First arrival

DOWN
1 "Take ___ breath"
2 Swiss cheese
3 Cry just before a rabbit appears?
4 Dwells in the past?
5 So, so long
6 Feminine side

7 Extraordinary
8 Red-spotted ___
9 Singer of the Wagner aria "Liebestod"
10 Be a breadwinner
11 Detective's work record
12 Either 17- or 57-Across
13 Snake's warning
15 3.3 in a transcript, maybe
21 Lead from a mountain?
23 Brickmaking need
25 Women of Andalucía: Abbr.
27 Drs.' org.
28 With clammy hands, say
30 N.Y.C. airport

32 Gymnastics coach Károlyi
33 Possible title for this puzzle
34 Deep discounts
36 Britain's Royal ___ Club, for plane enthusiasts
37 1051, on a monument
40 Complete the I.R.S.'s Schedule A
43 ___ fog
44 Bob at the Olympics
46 Puzzled
47 Dig, with "on"
48 Servings at teas
50 Doyenne
52 Like L-O-N-D-O-N
54 100-lb. units
55 Bear's warning
56 Simile center
58 Flashed sign

by Elizabeth C. Gorski

ACROSS

1 "A peculiar sort of a gal," in song
4 Muddy
8 Themed events
13 Actor Tognazzi of "La Cage aux Folles"
14 Seaside raptor
15 Allen Iverson's teammates till '06
16 Ingredient in some gum
18 Gossip
19 Request that often follows "Please"
20 Inceptions
21 Chow
22 Oscar Wilde or Bill Maher, for example
25 Some car roofs
27 Like some announcements that have been lost
28 Sister who's won the U.S. Open three times
30 Grafton's "___ for Innocent"
31 Curly shape
32 Starts of some games . . . and of the answers to 16-, 22-, 48- and 56-Across?
36 R.B.I. producer, sometimes: Abbr.
39 Holder of le trône
40 Minnesota college
44 "Hold on!"
47 Hot, after "on"
48 Like some passes
51 Mambo king Puente
52 Contravenes
53 They give you control
55 Fang
56 Cedar and hemlock
57 Lightly sprayed
58 Mathematician Post or Artin
59 Riddle-me-___
60 Foreign thoughts
61 Kind of column
62 New Left org.

DOWN

1 Hackneyed movie endings
2 Perturb
3 G.P.S. device, e.g.
4 Part of AARP: Abbr.
5 Small African antelope
6 "Back ___" (1974 Genesis song)
7 Family name of about 15% of Koreans
8 Big bomb
9 Runs out
10 Having a dividing wall, in biology
11 Locks
12 Map abbr. until 1991
15 TV Guide info
17 How many writers work
20 Buck ___, first black coach in Major League Baseball (Cubs, 1962)
23 Opening
24 Patriot's concerns, briefly
26 ___-Cat
29 What machmeters measure
33 Songs from rosy-cheeked singers, maybe
34 Moms and dads belong to it: Abbr.
35 Rather
36 Bad record, for short
37 Not a long-term solution
38 Certain plate
41 Overstays?
42 Not the same anymore
43 Gets ready to brush, maybe
45 This evening, on posters
46 Organic compounds with nitrogen
49 Step heavily (on)
50 Start of a counting rhyme
54 Like Clark Kent's manner
55 Third year in the reign of Edward the Elder
56 Corp. honcho

by Patrick McIntyre

The New York Times

SMART PUZZLES

Presented with Style

 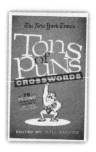  

Available at your local bookstore or online at www.nytimes.com/nytstore

🎔 St. Martin's Griffin

f facebook.com/NewYorkTimesCrosswordPuzzle

1

DOOR PRIM TAMPA
ALSO LENO ONEAL
MALT ASTO STAID
EVOCATION TINGE
LES TASTER
SCOPE THIRD
ALLIES EQUALITY
FADE MIDST AROO
EMERGING HAZARD
ARNEL PENTA
REMARK OSO
ALARM EQUIPPING
JESSE RUNT AVON
ANTON MAGI RAGA
HASNT ADEN KNOW

2

ROMP TUBAS CHIC
UNTO INERT OATH
NEWS NOLTE URSA
INTEND FROGMAN
NOFREELAUNCH
TROLL AETNA
EMMA BOO OLDIES
BEATTOTHEPAUNCH
BOLLIX ACE POKE
SWEET SOUND
IHAVEAHAUNCH
CATSEYE ONSALE
ALOU ELIHU AVID
STIR ATLAS GANG
HOLE REESE ELKE

3

GEWGAW SMOG BAM
ICEAGE LOOM UTE
BRIDALPATHS SRO
BURG FETE THAW
ERAS TOWEL
ALTAREDSTATES
ARE VETO TYRANT
HENRI AGO WAGER
ACTION INCA URI
AISLEBEDARNED
LEICA UNDO
MASS ROTC OONA
AMO MARRYANDREW
YOU ODES NELLIE
ASP SOLO STEELS

4

APSE CAROL OSLO
COIL AMANA UPON
DOZENDOZEN TARS
CREME READ LIRE
EAVE CABINET
TURNTO BRUINS
ABUT TARO DEPOT
LEM GENESIS ALI
CROCE NEST MIEN
RANCID STINGY
FORSALE SAKS
UHUH AHEM OCOME
DAME SATINSATIN
GROW PLUTO SILO
EARS SLIER TSKS

5

TENOR FLOP CHAP
ABABA ROSE HAVE
RAYOFLIGHT ANON
ONSITE SEALSKIN
SEGA ALE ODE
MANTRAPS SELF
ALI STATS REHAB
MACE ORATE SAGA
ANKLE TRESS ION
OILS RECHARGE
ARF LUG PURR
GETTABLE DITHER
OBIE BILLOFFARE
RIME EDIE TULSA
ADEN DEAN SLEEP

6

AHS SABRE BUCKO
REC IMEAN UNHIP
AIR NOAHCOMMENT
BRACKETS CRAZES
PLEBE BEAN
SAHARANWRAP WAH
PRESS RUN GERE
IDAS GRITS UIES
COPY LOS SIGNS
ERS TICTACTAHOE
PUNK BLUNT
ABOARD ALANALDA
LEFTBAHRAIN OUR
FRITO TORRE SET
ANTIS SNEER STY

7

```
H E R E ▮ A C U T E ▮ G R O G
A M E X ▮ N O S I R ▮ L I M O
I M N O T G O I N G T O P A Y
G A T ▮ A L G A E ▮ A R E N A
▮ ▮ A S E A ▮ ▮ S U I ▮ ▮ ▮
S H O R T E N T H E P A N T S
T E S T Y ▮ ▮ H A R E ▮ O A K
R A C Y ▮ H B O M B ▮ T I K I
E V A ▮ D A R N ▮ ▮ P O S E R
W E R E I N A G R E E M E N T
▮ ▮ ▮ N A G ▮ ▮ E L S E ▮ ▮
F E I G N ▮ K A P U T ▮ I D A
I M S E E I N G A D O C T O R
F I L L ▮ N O R S E ▮ A C M E
I R E S ▮ S W A T S ▮ W H O A
```

8

```
A M A T I ▮ S U I T ▮ Q U I P
S A L O N ▮ O H N O ▮ U R B S
T R A C T ▮ P U L P ▮ I D E S
I K N O W A S H O R T C U T ▮
▮ ▮ ▮ M O M ▮ ▮ W O R K ▮ ▮
F E T E ▮ B R A ▮ W O O D S Y
L A O ▮ D I A L S ▮ U N I T E
I T S N O T P L U G G E D I N
T A C O S ▮ T O R A H ▮ T E T
S T A T I C ▮ W E B ▮ H O S E
▮ ▮ A D E E ▮ ▮ O O O ▮ ▮ ▮
▮ M Y B O S S W O N T M I N D
S O S O ▮ S T A R ▮ H A N O I
E L E V ▮ N E N E ▮ E G R E T
W E R E ▮ A R T S ▮ R E E L S
```

9

```
S U M A C ▮ J E T S ▮ P O E T
I T A L O ▮ O B I T ▮ O S L O
P E R T H ▮ N A N A ▮ W R E N
▮ T H E R I Y A L T H I N G
▮ E I E I O ▮ ▮ A C A C I A
D I N A R A T E I G H T ▮ ▮
O L E ▮ S N E A D ▮ R A P I D
H A T H ▮ S A R I S ▮ N O D E
A T S E A ▮ S L O O P ▮ N E W
▮ ▮ R U P E E T U E S D A Y
A L K A L I ▮ ▮ N O T E S ▮
G U I L D E R R A D N E R ▮
L E N D ▮ R O A R ▮ I R O N Y
O G E E ▮ C A N T ▮ E N S U E
W O R D ▮ E D D Y ▮ S A A B S
```

10

```
C A S T ▮ A D A M S ▮ D A Z E
A C T A ▮ F R A I L ▮ O K A Y
P R O M ▮ F O R M A ▮ C A P E
P E P P E R W E I G H T ▮ ▮
▮ ▮ ▮ S A N ▮ ▮ B O S C S
C A V I T Y ▮ A B N O R M A L
A R O S E ▮ P L I E ▮ E R A
P E T E R P O L L E N M A R Y
O N E ▮ ▮ I L I E ▮ E E R I E
T A R R A G O N ▮ T E A S E R
E S S E N ▮ ▮ B A D ▮ ▮ ▮
▮ ▮ E I G H T I S S N U F F
J A I L ▮ R O O T S ▮ O G L E
A X L E ▮ A B A T E ▮ S L O T
W E L D ▮ M O D E L ▮ H Y P E
```

11

```
G C L E F ▮ F L O E ▮ S H E D
I R A T E ▮ L O O K ▮ H O P E
G O W H E R E T H E I O N I S
S P A N ▮ H A T ▮ O N D E C K
▮ ▮ B I B I ▮ C U T ▮ ▮ ▮
P R I C I N G C A T H O L I C
L A D ▮ D O R I C ▮ E L I S E
A D I N ▮ S U L K S ▮ E V A N
T I N T S ▮ M I L E R ▮ E A T
H I G H I M P A E R O B I C S
▮ ▮ ▮ T O Y ▮ ▮ G M E N ▮
D R A W U P ▮ R O E ▮ A M A S
D I S A P P E A R I N G A C T
A S I S ▮ E V I L ▮ A L I N E
Y E A H ▮ D E N Y ▮ B E D E W
```

12

```
R O C K Y ▮ D R O P ▮ M E L T
I N A N E ▮ R A V E ▮ A P E R
B E S O T ▮ A G E E ▮ R O V E
▮ S T I C K E R P R I C E S
C H E ▮ O E D ▮ H A S H E S
H A T R E D ▮ ▮ F O E ▮ ▮
A R T I N ▮ F O O L ▮ I D E A
F E E S C H A R G E D B Y A N
E S S E ▮ A I R Y ▮ D I N G O
▮ ▮ ▮ E R R ▮ ▮ M E D A L S
S E N E C A ▮ S K I ▮ S E E
A C U P U N C T U R I S T ▮
W O R E ▮ G O A D ▮ T A I L S
E L S E ▮ U P T O ▮ C R E E L
D I E S ▮ E Y E S ▮ H A S T Y
```

13

```
M O N S . . G A O L . . S Y N E
A M A H . L E N T O . . H O O D
L E G O M U T T O N . . A G E D
A G A W A M . S E G O L I L Y .
R A T E D P G . . O R O . . . .
. . . D A Y O J U D G M E N T .
A L B U M . T A N D Y . D E Y .
P E R P . W H I P S . Y E A R .
E V A . C H I M E . R A N T O .
R I G H T O C E N T E R . . . .
. . I N C . . S O L D I E R . .
F A I L S A F E . D I A N N E .
E L A L . R I N G O T R U T H .
E D G E . E L V E S . M I R E .
T O O L . S L Y E . . S T E M .
```

14

```
C L O G S . O L E S . . J I F F
H O V E L . D E B T . . E D I E
A G A N A . O V E R . . D O N E
D E L I V E R Y R E V I L E D .
. . . E E L . . T A I . . . . .
C B S . S E M I . . M O S T E L
H O P I . N O D E . L O R R E .
E R O S S A W I W A S S O R E .
S N O O P . N O E L . A T O Z .
T E N N I S . T R I G . S R A .
. . R I A . . E O S . . . . . .
P A R T O N D I D N O T R A P .
O M A R . K O B E . . G R A V E
P A C E . E R I N . . O A T E S
S T Y X . R E S T . . O P A R T
```

15

```
F A K E . L A M B S . . F U M E
A R A L . A N N I E . . I B A R
T U R K E Y T O R T . D E L I .
A B A . V E E . C O T E R I E .
L A T H E R . C H U R L . . . .
. . E R I C A . T I C K L E . .
D I A L . N U T S . M A N I A .
A C R E . G R E E R . S E A R .
M E A N S . T R E E . T E R N .
P T B O A T . E R A T O . . . .
. . F L O O D . S E R A P E . .
F L A T T O P . D O N . G O D .
L O G O . L E M O N D O R P S .
A L A R . E R A S E . P E P E .
W A R Y . D A T E R . T E A L .
```

16

```
S H A M A N . . C H A P E L .
H O S A N N A . C H A L I C E
I W O N D E R W H E R E T H E
P E K E S . T A O . E T H O S
. . D O C U D R A M A . . . .
A M F . A R I E L . . T A E .
M A E S T R O . S I M M O N S
M O T H E R . . B E A R I S .
A R C A D E S . G A G R U L E
N I H . R E H A B . . S S S .
. . I C E P A L A C E . . . .
A V I L A . A N O . O N E I S
F A M O U S L A S T W O R D S
O N A S S I S . H E L L I O N
R E N T E R . . A S S E S S .
```

17

```
P E T S . A J A R . A M O R E
O L E O . S E X Y . R O L E X
T E N N I S S E E . E D I C T
A M S . N A T . I N E V E R .
T E E N S Y . F L O O R I D A
O N D I T . S O O N . N A E S
. T U N A . L O U I S . . . .
. P E N C I L V A N I A . . .
. . T A P I R . O R I G . . .
S T E R . N O N E . W A R E S
W H Y O M I N G . A D E S T E
I R E N E S . B R A . P I A .
V I L A S . M A R R Y L A N D
E V I L S . O L I O . O C T O
T E D D Y . B L O W . G E O G
```

18

```
B E A S T . O S C A R . T A G
A D L A I . C A R P E . O I L
B U G S P R A Y E R S . A D O
A C E . T U T . P O T S D A M
S E R M O N . C E N S E S . .
. . T E S L A . S T I T C H .
C A S S . T O T S . O S O L E
U G H . C O W S L I P . O A R
P R E G O . E C O N . E L M O
S I E R R A . A G A P E . . .
. . P A S S O N . W A L K B Y
P O S S E S S . L A B . N R A
I R K . T U R K E Y S H O O T
E L I . E R I K A . T O W N E
S Y N . D E C K S . S Y N C S
```

19

```
PROB  SAWS  BEFIT
RENI  EXIT  ERICA
IDIG  MONA  ROREM
SHOOTINGRANGE
MONTH     NEEDNT
STY RATIFY NEAR
  DOTODO SOPPY
 BREAKINGOUT
PRAYS YODELS
ABCS POTATO BUN
LIKESO   NURSE
 BATTERINGRAMS
PROSE RUDE GNAT
CANOE AMEX EDIE
SPEND SPAT SOLD
```

20

```
CAMP  SWEAT  BAAL
BRAE  LARCH  ACRE
SEND  ICIER  ZAGS
 DIAMONDOFACES
ORACLE   ELAINE
NOMAS SAM ORATE
CLUBOFKNAVES
ELS DITCH KAI
 SPADEOFKINGS
APACE SSN ACORN
GARAND  GNAWAT
HEARTOFQUEENS
ALGA ROUSE SHOE
SLOB ARIES EONS
TANS LAPSE EWES
```

21

```
OJOS  IOTAS  ZAHN
ROPE  BRANT  OBIE
CUTTINGCORONERS
ARSON TRICKLES
 NEMO AKA
WAG REDSKELETON
ELECTRIC AMORE
BITO SNOBS MALT
TBARS POLKADOT
VITALOREGON SPY
 URE STOP
SUBURBIA WHIFF
SHOPPINGSENATOR
RUNT TIEIN SERA
SHOO SNERD EMMY
```

22

```
SILAS  ALFA  RILE
KNELT  RIAL  EDEN
IFYOUWANTLIFETO
RUDE ACE CRASS
TSE GRAMERCY
SENOR RARE ASA
 BEGINATFORTY
AWEIGH CANCAN
DONTGOEIGHTY
DOE SAGA EXAMS
 PETUNIAS TAP
ETHEL OTT DORA
WHENYOURETWENTY
ERIC USER HECHE
SURE RODS OREAD
```

23

```
VCR  PATTI  KEFIR
IRA  OLEAN  OXIDE
SAC  NORTH  VALET
AMEDIUMSOCALLED
SPREE   TACT
 LSATS TSETSE
BECAUSEIT DEAN
USA PERSONA CST
NARC ISNEITHER
KIBOSH YOURE
 RUMP PERCH
RARENORWELLDONE
ABOLT MANIA MOW
TESLA ACTON ATE
STAIN NOONE NED
```

24

```
ITSA  MARS  MATZO
BRIC  ALOT  ANION
AUNTIEEMU NANNY
RECURS ANON TEX
 DEARTH TRIG
 LEROI ASLEEP
JAM GOLDENHINDU
OLEO DAD BONN
SAMTHESHAMU SAY
EROTIC OMENS
 ONCE STITCH
BOZ TELL ITALIA
ORIBI BOGEYMENU
SATIN OVER PAGE
SLING WETS STER
```

25

```
F I A T S █ J I L L █ R U B E
A N G I E █ I D E A █ U S E R
C H A S E C H E V Y █ S U E R
E O N █ D R A M █ E T H A N E
S T A B B E D █ S T A B L E D
█ █ E E E █ S U T R A █ █ █
F I E N D S █ A N E █ R O A D
A W A C S █ I N K █ A B A C I
B O T H █ I R T █ A W A K E N
█ █ J A C K O █ W A R █ █ █
R E S O L E S █ G A R A G E S
A L T H E A █ A R I D █ A L P
T U R N █ G O R E T I P P E R
E D E N █ E R L E █ N I E C E
D E W Y █ S O O N █ G E S T E
```

26

```
W I N S █ S I G M A █ S P A M
A S E A █ P L E A D █ M A X I
L O W [TURN] S R I N G S █ A G E D
T U T O R I A L █ █ A R E █
█ R O U T E D █ D O N T [TURN] E R
█ █ T A R █ D A L I █ B E E
P O L S █ W A N E S █ A R N
A B E █ J O H N D O E █ C I D
R E F █ A M I T Y █ E K E S
E S T █ P E T E █ S Y N █
R E [TURN] L A N E █ U T A H A N
█ █ T O N █ O P E R A H A T
T H O U █ N O C [TURN] E D N O S E
A M O S █ O N T A P █ C O T E
D O Z E █ D E A L S █ E T Y M
```

27

```
C A C T I █ M A N D M █ G A P
U B O A T █ A L O N E █ E M U
B E E T S A M P R A S █ N E T
█ █ S O L E S █ S P E N T
B O O █ P A T █ M A K E S D O
A N K L E S █ Z E N I T H █
S I R E N █ M O T E T █ A M A
I C A N █ S I N E W █ S L A B
L E W █ H A T E R █ J U L I A
█ I M A G E S █ C A N O N S
F U N N I E S █ M A Y █ T E E
I N F O R █ F A I L S █
F I R █ P A U L I N E K A L E
E T E █ I R K E D █ N I G E L
R E Y █ N E E D S █ O N E A L
```

28

```
A S E C █ A G F A █ O N I C E
M E S A █ F L E X █ N Y L O N
A R A L █ R E A L █ E M E N D
J A I L S E N T E N C E █ █
█ █ E I S █ L E T S B E
F O U R T H D I M E N S I O N
E R N I E █ E B E R T █ S R S
L A R D █ F T E N S █ L I E U
I T I █ A R E A S █ V I S O R
P O P U L A R M A G A Z I N E
E R E S T U █ █ A L P █
█ █ T E S T E R S S H O U T
A S F O R █ E X I T █ A N T I
V A L U E █ R A G A █ I M I N
E C A R D █ I M A X █ R E L Y
```

29

```
M A R A T █ C A R O M █ A T M
A T A R I █ A R O A R █ R O I
C O M I C A C T O R S █ M O M
R O I L █ L A O S █ C C C L I
O T S █ S M O O T █ R A H
█ █ T O A █ C A M A R O
A S S O C █ I M H O T █ I O S
A C H R I S T M A S C A R O L
H O I █ A T O M S █ H A S T O
S T R O L L █ A I R █
█ T L C █ S H A L T █ C A L
T O T A L █ M A S T █ C A L I
A R A █ A L A S T A I R S I M
T A I █ S O L T I █ M A C A O
A L L █ S O L A R █ A M A S S
```

30

```
B U T T I N █ J A R S █ U S E
B R A W N Y █ A B E L █ N E A
C U B E D T O M A T O █ Z I G
█ L E I █ L I R A █ S I Z E
P R E █ G R E E N P E P P E R
L A S S O E S █ E L O █ █
A N A T █ S T O P █ M O M M A
C I L A N T R O O R O N I O N
E N T R E █ A M M O █ E L L O
█ █ T H O █ A W A R D E D
C H I L I P O W D E R █ S S E
R O V E █ T R E E █ C P A
O V O █ D I C E D G A R L I C
P E R █ O M A N █ O D E S S A
S L Y █ E A S Y █ P E T A R D
```

31

```
P A S S E D U P ■ S T U P I D
A R T U R O T O S C A N I N I
C L E R I C A L C O L L A R S
M E R G E ■ H A I R L I N E S
A N N E ■ C A R O N ■ M O P E
N E O ■ F O G I N ■ N I K O N
■ ■ N A M E S ■ C U T E S T
M A D I G A N ■ S A D E Y E S
C L O N E S ■ D O M E D ■ ■
E G G O N ■ L O C U S ■ M U D
N E W T ■ H U L K S ■ T I L E
T R A C T A B L E ■ P U N T S
I N T H E N E A R F U T U R E
R O C K A N D R O L L S T A R
E N H A L O ■ S O U P I E S T
```

32

```
O T T O ■ S P R A N G ■ C A D
N E O N ■ H O A G I E ■ I R R
E R R S ■ E N F A N T ■ G T E
S E E P ■ L E A S E S ■ A U S
E S S E ■ ■ E S A U ■ R R S
C A T C H A G L I M P S E O F
■ ■ ■ I C U ■ ■ ■ E T T O
L E A G U E ■ E R E C T O R
O U G H T S ■ R E P R E S S
G R A T E S ■ I L I E S C U
■ ■ A A A ■ ■ ■ T M A C
S E E I N G E Y E ■ C O N C
T O L L G A T E S ■ O K I E
R E S I L I E N T ■ D E N S
■ ■ T E N ■ ■ ■ E R I S
```

33

```
C O M P A R E D A G A I N S T
A T O O T H F O R A T O O T H
T R U E T O T H E L E T T E R
S A D T O ■ ■ ■ N A C R E
U N A S ■ H A I R S ■ S O I E
P T L ■ B O T N E T S ■ O L A
S O L V E T H E P R O B L E M
■ ■ I N T E R L U D E ■ ■
I M M E D I A T E D A N G E R
C E O ■ S P R I T E S ■ E R E
E R R S ■ S T A E L ■ P R O M
B I D O N ■ ■ ■ A I M T O
A M E R I C A N T A B L O I D
G E N E R A L A U D I E N C E
S E T S O N A P E D E S T A L
```

34

```
B A T H ■ T R E A T ■ S H O D
A F R O ■ N O R T H ■ I O W A
S O O T ■ O U N C E ■ X M E N
R O U L E T T E ■ C H E E S E
A T T I M E S ■ B R A S S ■
■ ■ N U S ■ A R O O ■ T A M
A P S E ■ C R A W L ■ E L M
B A L S A ■ O S U ■ E V A D E
I C E ■ B A C O N ■ I D O S
T E E ■ L R O N ■ T E L ■
■ P O E M A ■ V E R I S M O
P A S T R Y ■ M A N O F W A R
A L O T ■ A R O M A ■ I A N A
C A F E ■ N I N O N ■ E M I T
T S A R ■ T O A S T ■ R I C E
```

35

```
B I O L ■ B O S C H ■ M A C E
R A R E ■ O R T H O ■ A L A S
E M A G ■ B R E E D S H I L L
A N N U L S ■ W A S H O ■ ■
D O G M A ■ S A P ■ A G A T E
S T E E R ■ T R O U ■ A L M A
■ ■ E D I T ■ T E N D E R
E C U A D O R ■ M A R Y A N N
G A S L O G ■ A S H E ■ ■
A R I L ■ S E V E ■ S H E E P
L E A S T ■ M O C ■ T I L D E
■ ■ I O N I C ■ R U D E S T
N E W Z E A L A N D ■ E V E S
F R E E ■ S I D E A ■ H E L I
L A B S ■ H O O T S ■ I N S T
```

36

```
■ H A M L E T ■ D E I S T S
P O S T U R E ■ R E S O R T S
I N T A I L S ■ A L L R I S E
C O O P S ■ T A W ■ A B B I E
A R L O ■ F S L I C ■ S U M P
R E A ■ A L I E N O R ■ T O E
D E T O N A T E ■ L E G E N D
■ ■ P E T E ■ R O S E ■ ■
H I T S A T ■ M O R E L A N D
E O E ■ R A R E B I T ■ I E R
A D M S ■ X E N O N ■ A L A E
P I P E T ■ C U T ■ I G E T A
E D U A R D O ■ I G N O R E D
D E R N I E R ■ C I T R O N S
■ S A S S E D ■ S L O A N S
```

37

```
E E E E . M A Y . Q Q Q Q
M E D E A . A T V . C U T I T
F O U R L E T T E R W O R D S
. . . I I I I . T T T T . . .
. S S E . G N A T S . I M S .
G E T S T H E R E . S N E E R
O N E T O T E N . J I G G L E
O O P . A H S . F A N . A L A
D R O I D S . G A N G S T E R
S A U C Y . A N C E S T O R S
. S T E . A R C E D . O N S .
. . . B B B B . O O O O . . .
R E P E A T O F F E N D E R S
I N E R T . R E F . A B D U L
G G G G . . S Y S . . Y Y Y Y
```

38

```
R I P S A W S . B A T T E A U
A N T I D E P R E S S A N T S
I S O L A T I O N B O O T H S
L U L L S . C O D A S . R O T
C R E S . N U K E D . N E U E
A R M . H O L E D . C O P S E
R E A S O N E D . N E U R A L
. C I T I E S . S E N S E N .
A T C O S T . N I N T E N D O
T I S N T . M O D E S . E A R
L O Y E . P O S E S . M U N I
U N S . S A L A D . T A R D E
N A T I O N A L I Z A T I O N
C R E A S E R E S I S T A N T
H Y M N A L S . H A S S L E S
```

39

```
E C R U . G L A S S . T E E M
A L U M . S I N A I . E M M A
N O T B Y A L O N G . E M I R
. S A R A . . T N T . E L I .
L E B A N O N . A S H O T I N
A D A . G U A M . . A U T O .
G I G A . I M E A N I T . . .
S N A P . J E L L O . D O W N
. . H O A R D E R . O C H O .
. S H I P . . S U V S . C I G
T H E D A R K . T O P H A T S
H U T . H A N . . E A S E . .
U T E P . G U N W E D D I N G
G U R U . A R O A R . J O E L
S P O T . S L I N G . I N D O
```

40

```
E S S O . A B A . . D R I E D
L E E S . C A T . S O O N Y I
B A A L . C A T . P O S H E R
A L L O U T . N O A H S A R K
. . . . L S D . T R A I L . .
C A F F E . O F T E N . A H H
O H A R E . C L E M . I T O O
M O L E . S T O R E . L I R R
M O L E . C O O P . F L O S S
A T E . G O R D O . R E N E E
. . N E A T O . P B A . . . .
T W O B Y T W O . A N I M A L
R I V O L I . D O G . T C B Y
A D E L I E . D O G . L I O N
M E R I T . . S H Y . L I O N
```

41

```
G E O M E T R I C S E R I E S
A C T I V E I N T E R E S T S
T H E D E S C E N T O F M A N
S T A I N L E S S S T E E L S
. . . . T A R . . F I R . . .
R A J A H S . L A R C . O W S
O Z O N E . E A S E . T R A P
Y O U K N O W T H E D R I L L
A L L A . P O K Y . A I O L I
L E E . J A K E . C Y G N E T
. . . J A R . . F O B . . . .
E S S E N T I A L O R G A N S
T E L L S I T L I K E I T I S
R E A L E S T A T E A G E N T
E D M O N T O N E S K I M O S
```

42

```
L A L . C A M A C H O . A G O
A G A . H A R S H E R . M O W
B L O W O U T T I R E S A L E
F E T E . . O N B O A R D . .
E A S T M A N . A S S A I L S
E M E R I T U S . . B L E U
. . . A R A B I A N S . L A R
L I N G E R I E H A L F O F F
A N A . D I A G O N A L . . .
C P U S . . E M A N A T E S
T U T O R E D . E S T I V A L
. B I P O L A R . . R S T U
A L L S U I T S S L A S H E D
L I U . T H E V I E W . O R G
P C S . S U R P L U S . W Y E
```

43

```
P A L P S ■ A R A B ■ A M P M
A L I A S ■ L O D E S T A R S
R E B U T ■ D I D G E R[IDO]O S
T V[IDO]L ■ P A S S E D O F F ■
V E S S E L ■ ■ T O P H A T
■ O K A P I S ■ N O O N E
■ W I N E C A S K ■ A S N E R
S O P ■ [IDO][IDO][IDO][IDO][IDO] ■ O R R
T R U S S ■ F R O T H E R S ■
A T R I A ■ F A S T E R ■
C H I L[IDO]G ■ E N R A P T
■ A T E K O S H E R ■ A S E A
P L A N T F O O D ■ S T A R R
P O N T O O N E D ■ H U M[IDO]R
S T I R ■ R O S Y ■ A M I T Y
```

44

```
D I S C ■ F L A V O R F L A V
E L L A ■ I A M A M E R I C A
F L O R ■ S P I C E G I R L S
■ S W E E T D E A L ■ T A U T
■ M E L B A ■ S E A T ■
I R O N L U N G ■ T R A M P S
P A T ■ Y M C A S ■ S T R U T
A S I A ■ P E L E G ■ A S T O
S T O U T ■ S A N E R ■ P T L
S A N T A S ■ S T T E R E S A
■ O P A H ■ I O N I A ■
N A O H ■ L A T E L U N C H
I N L A L A L A N D ■ S O A P
B A D R O M A N C E ■ E C H O
S T E P S I S T E R ■ S K A T
```

45

```
S E T U P ■ S A P O R ■ E T E
A D O R E ■ N U R S E ■ C O L
F I R S T L A D I E S ■ O N O
E T N A ■ E P I C ■ F L I P
■ S T A T E P O L I C E ■
■ E L D E S T ■ T A R O ■
S L O O P ■ H A N G O V E R
H E R O ■ M O O G S ■ R A V E
O V E R H A N G ■ S I N E W
■ D I C E ■ L E T T E R ■
P O L I C E S T A T E ■
E R I E ■ I R M A ■ L O I S
T A N ■ L A D I E S F I R S T
A T E ■ A B E T S ■ E S T E E
L E S ■ C A D E T ■ U P S E T
```

46

```
S S T ■ H A N ■ T H E F A R S
I L O V E L A ■ H I B A C H I
D E V I C E S ■ R E B A T E D
E W A L K S A L E ■ ■ E O E
■ S H E L ■ H E A V Y ■
■ S E R T A ■ S T A T E S
S E C T ■ O H S ■ K E N O B I
I R R ■ H E X A G O N ■ G O D
D O O W O P ■ A P U ■ M A N E
E S W I P E ■ P A T T I ■
■ T I R E S ■ I D D O
S K A ■ M O U N T A I N S
I N S P I R E ■ S A L I E R I
D E T E N T E ■ E M E R G E D
E W I N D E R ■ D E S ■ O D E
```

47

```
● P U N C H ■ P E N D ■ A A A
C A S T L E ■ I G O R ■ C S I
A Y E S I R ■ N O M A T T E R
R E T ■ P O T ●S ■ P O S T ●
D R O P P E R S ■ F E R N
■ D E S I ■ O R N A T E
R A D A R ■ P R O X Y ■ I R A
A M I S ■ L O O P ● ■ O V E R
T B A ■ S I D E A ■ K N E E ●
● I N O N E ■ Q U I Z ■
■ A X O N ■ S U P R E M E S
P A R E R ■ N I E L S ■ R Y E
I R O N E D O N ■ A T T L E E
A M S ■ R I S K ■ N I N E ● S
F ● S ■ S P Y ● ■ D E T E S T
```

48

```
G A P I N G ■ C L A R A B O W
O N E P E R ■ N O S E D I V E
O T T A W A ■ T A K E S T E A
D I S S ■ D I O D E S ■ E R R
G E T S ■ U N W E D ■ B O D E
A T O ■ B A K E D ■ M A N O R
M A R K E T E R ■ F E B ■
E M E R G E D ■ P L A Y S O N
■ O E D ■ M A I N M E N U
F A I N T ■ R I V E T ■ A B C
O N M E ■ S O N E S ■ S H U L
R A P ■ I N C U R S ■ C O T E
O K E Y D O K E ■ O P O R T O
N I N E I R O N ■ L A W S O N
E N D T O E N D ■ O L S E N S
```

49

```
A R I A # O R V A L # I N K Y
M A W R # N A I V E # N O N E
T H A T R E M A I N S S E E N
# N Y E T # # E T O I L E S #
O P T # B O R N W I L D # # #
N R A # A T E E # L U E L L A
B E L # W A S T # T R U E S #
A M O # N O T T O B E # C S I
S I N G E # A L K Y # K I A #
E X E R T S # E A R S # Y O N
# # I T H A D Y O U # A N S #
P A M E L A S # N E I L # # #
Y O U V E G O T K I D D I N G
R U N E # G R I T S # O V E R
O T I S # Y E A S T # L E E R
```

50

```
P A P A # S H A S T A # I V Y
O P U S # T O R P O R # F A A
W I R Y # A E R A T E # N C O
W E S L E [YIN/YANG] R A D U A T E # #
O C E A N # # Y E P # R E B A
W E D # D N A # # F I D E L #
# # A L Y S S A # R A B B I #
# D I R E C T E D B [YIN/YANG] L E E #
S I M M S # I N R A G S # # #
A R I A S # # Y A P # T R E #
P E N N # T H A # A S H E N #
# L I B [YIN/YANG] O V E R N M E N T
A D O # I G N O R E # A F A R
N O V # N U D I S M # C A M E
T E E # S P A R E S # K N E E
```

51

```
P I T C H Y # # C I C A D A S
I N R O A D # O L D K N I C K
S K I L L S # G O E S I N T O
A S C O T # E R D A # # G O R
# K N E W T E S T A M E N T #
# # D O C # E T E # # # #
B R E W # L E W D # T R E S S
L A D Y O F T H E K N I G H T
U S U A L # C A F E # T O Y S
# # T A N # E N O # # # #
K N O T F O R P R O F I T #
I O S # W O E S # F L I E S
C O M E L A T E # C A L L M E
K N I T P I C K # T I E D U P
S E C A N T S # # A R R E S T
```

52

```
B A N J O # L O C A L # M U M
O C E A N # O C H R E # E N O
F R U S T R A T I O N # N P R
F E T C H E D # A G A T E S #
# # H E X # M O R T G A G E #
A C T A S # S U R # H A L #
M O E # L E T S G O # I N K S
I T M A Y B E T A K E N O U T
E S P N # B L A N D A # T H E
# T I X # M R S # S T E N T
F A S T F O O D # S T R # #
U N F A I R # M E L I N D A
N I A # L I B R A R Y B O O K
G O T # E B O N Y # M A I Z E
O N E # S I N A I # E L R E Y
```

53

```
N I N E # O L A N # P A S S E
O N O R # T I N E # E M P T Y
L A M A # T O N E # S M I T E
E T A S # O N U S # T O R E #
S I N E W # L O G # I R A
S E S S I L E # N A P S T E R
# # # S O R E # L A T E S T
S T A N D A R D W O R K D A Y
P E R I O D # S O R T # #
I S T H M U S # P E E V I S H
N T H # P C B # D O L C E
# F O R T # O R B S # I L E X
C L U E R # F O R E # D I N O
O E S T E # F I R E # O N E S
S W E D E # S L R S # F I V E
```

54

```
A P E R S # S I R E # R E P
R O D E O # I N N E R # A G E
R I D D L E C A K E S # I R A
# # T I M O R # K E R N E L
M I R A # I N L A W # C A T S
O N A P A R # L E G A L # #
N A V E L # M O T E L # C A M
E N E # P R O V O K E # O R E
T E N # H U L A S # A S H E N
# I P A N A # S N O O T S
A L M A # T R A L A # P L E A
M E A D O W # L I N E R # #
B A G # R O W I N G P A I N S
E V E # C R A C K # I N D I E
R E S # S K Y E # C O O P T
```

55

```
A R C S   C E L S   S C A R F
T E R I   E X I T   A L F I E
O N A N   D U N E   B A T O N
M O N G R E L E M P I R E
I I I   E S T   O N E R U N
C R A W L   P A L   T Y N E
  A I L   A M I D   O U T
  C U R C U R R I C U L U M
A L L   S T E T   E C O
M A T T   I C Y   K N O B S
O D I O U S   P S I   L A P
  M U T T V I L L E N I N E
E N A C T   I D E A   I V A N
L A T H E   A L A N   T E N D
S T E E R   L E S T   E R A S
```

56

```
O D D   S H U   T A R   T O E
C A R L T O N   E X E G E T E
T H E L A R K   M I N E R A L
A L W A Y S I N P O E T R Y
    N S Y N C   M E S A
C O M O   D A G   A C I D
O V O   M O N A R C H T O B E
M E N   A W E   E A U   T O M
B R O N T E S J A N E   T O O
O T T O   S E T   Y A K S
  O B O E   S W A L E
  S N O B B I S H M A N N E R
F O O D I E S   I M I T A T E
G R U Y E R E   T A N L I N E
H E S   S T E   E N E   L A D
```

57

```
F A U N   C A J U N   S H A M
D U P E   I G O T A   H U G E
I T O O   S A L A D   O R E L
C O N N E C T T H E D O T S
    A L O E   R E I
S K A T E   S I R   V N E C K
I N S A N E   G P S   N O N
N O P L A C E L I K E H O M E
G T E   O X O   I N A L I E
A S N E R   C O D   I M A C S
    S A D   O M A R
  A L P H A B E T I C A L L Y
C Z A R   C A V I L   D I E U
A U D I   C R E M E   I S A K
P L A T   A B N E R   O A F S
```

58

```
O M E N   G L I B   S S G T S
F O C I   R O L L   L E O N E
F O O T L O O S E   U N I O N
    P A W P A W P R I N T S
E S K I M O   A P O G E E
C A N C A N O P E N E R
L E A K S   R A N G E   S P A
A N C Y   R O L O S   S O O N
T S K   H A U E R   L O C K E
    T O M T O M T U R K E Y
E L A Y N E   E N C O R E
B O N B O N V O Y A G E
B R I A R   I N A M E R I C A
E C O L E   E C R U   E D N A
D A N T E   W E E P   R O N A
```

59

```
T H R E E M E N I N A B O A T
H O R N S O F A D I L E M M A
U R S U S   T M E N   B E A K
M T   R A I S E S   P O N T I
B O L E Y N   S I P   T N
N N E   E N S T A T E   R E G
A H A   D E P O S I T   E R L
I E R   R U R A L   M O I
L A N   M E R R I E R   A F B
S R S   C A T E R T O   I C E
K S   C A R   T A I L O R
E A T I N   S C R O D S   U T
T W O S   O P I E   H O U R I
C H O C O L A T E M O U S S E
H O N O R A R Y D E G R E E S
```

60

```
F O C A L   E P I C   R A S H
I N A N E   G A L A   E L M O
C U R V E B A L L S   D L I I
A S P I R I N   S E C R E T S
    L A B   D A Y L I G H T
C H E S T   B U Y   I V E Y
U R L   I O C   A M E
T H I N G S T H A T B R E A K
    E U R   E L M   P I T
  L A W S   E S L   T S A R S
K I D S T O Y S   E W E
L E A D O R E   G O O D O N E
E D G E   O C E A N W A V E S
I T I S   N U M B   A T E S T
N O O K   O P U S   Y E N T A
```

61

```
R I A L . S T Y X . H A L A S
E S T A . E A V E . A L A M O
C I T[YSL]I C K E R . R A D I I
U N L O O S E S . C H R[YSL]E R
S T E W S . . S A L A M I .
E O E . S C A L A R . P T S
. F A S H I O N . E P I C
P I G L A T I N . G R E T A
A N A I S . T I R E I R O N
C O L T . C O L O G N E .
E N L . S A T A N S . C A R
. E R E S T U . A K I T A
P A[YSL]I P S . R E S P E C T S
A P A C T . B E A U T[YSL]E E P
L E V E E . A N T E . O R N E
E X E R T . I T S Y . T O D D
```

62

```
B A D E . S P L I T . F O R E
A M E X . P L A Z A . I P O D
R U L E . R A Z O R . G E L S
B L A C K E Y E D P E A R Y .
S E N . N E E . S E R A P E
. T O N E . R T S . N O T O N
. . I A M . H I M . O L D
. G O L D E N A R C H E R Y .
R A N . T I N . S A G .
E L E N I . B E G . S O L D
C A P O N S . E A T . I U M
. C O R D U R O Y P A N T R Y
S T U D . M O R S E . A C H E
M I N I . P O S E R . S H A Y
A C D C . S T O R Y . T I M E
```

63

```
C A D S . C H A D . C R E S T
A W O L . R A R E . R O Y C E
G A Z A . E G O S . I C E A X
E Y E C L A U D I U S . T N T
. K I T E . A N I G H .
S L E E V E . C R I S P E R
W A Y N E . S A N O . O J A I
A P E . S O P R A N O . U N C
P E L E . L O D Z . S P R E E
. L I S T E N S . S T A Y E D
. K L E I G . P O E T .
A W E . A N E Y E F O R A N I
S H I P S . B U T T . O R E O
P E K O E . O L E O . L E A N
S T E E R . B E R N . S A L S
```

64

```
G R E W . A N(A)I S . L A B S
L A R A . N O[ST/AR]C H . E B O N
A N I L . E S T E E . A D U E
R A(C)K E T E E R S . (D)O L E
E T H O S . . . M E R
. F A M . R A P . L I V
C H E F . I R E N E . O N A N
C O L A . L O[ST/AR]T S . S A R S
S L A M . A T E S T . A L D A
. L I E . N E A . O W N .
A Y N . . . A G A T E
T W E(E) . V A M P I R E B A(T)
T O M A . E D U C T . L A S H
H O A R . R E[ST/AR]T S . E T T A
E D Y S . A N D S O . S E E N
```

65

```
A C D C . A M W A Y . H M O
S H O E . C U R B S . B O E R
P[IMP]L Y . A N I S E . L Y R A
. L O N G T E R M[IMP]A C T
S K[IMP]O N . B I N . O S S I E
T R A N S . E N T E R . .
E A S E . S A G . S E T U P S
M I S S I O N[IMP]O S S I B L E
S T E E D S . L B O . G O A T
. Y O D E L . [IMP]E A C H
G R A I L . E M I . E R T E S
L I T T L E D E V I L S .
[IMP]A L E . B U N I N . H E E L
S L A M . A C T O N . R A G U
E S S . Y E S N O . [IMP]R O V
```

66

```
C A L E B . E L M S . S T E P
T R I T E . N O A H . L I R A
S C A R E . T O R I . O A R S
. H O U S T O N C A S T R O S
. S W A M . . O H A R E
C H I C A G O C L U B S . .
R E L A X . L O O S E . A G O
E R I N . D O N N E . T R O D
W O E . R O G G E . A H E A D
. N E W Y O R K M E A T S
N I S E I . A I M S . .
E X P A N S I O N T E A M S
A N E T . L O N G . T U B E D
T A R E . A N T E . E C A R D
H Y M N . M O O R . R E S E T
```

67

```
[TURN] P  I  K  E  |  I  L  S  A  |  |  O  W  E  S
   K   I  R  I  N  |  O  A  K  S  |  |  K  O  N  A
   E   L  E  N  A  |  T  W  I  S  T  A  N  D [TURN]
   Y   O  N  |  B  R  A  D  B  U  R  Y  |
   |   T  E  S  L  A  |  Y  O  R  E  |  J  A  W
   |   W  E  D  S  |  B  E  S  E  E  C  H
   M   A  K  E  S  A  U [TURN] |  S  A  L  T  Y
   E   G  A  D  |  R  E [TURN] E  D  |  S  L  I  M
   R   A  Z  E  R  |  [TURN] T  O  S  T  O  N  E
   L   I  O  N  E  S  S  |  A  W  O  L  |
   E   N  O  |  T  O  O  K  |  S  P  A  I  N
   |   S  I  N  C  E  R  E  R  |  C  A  T
[TURN] I  N  G  P  O  I  N  T  |  A  L  A  M  O
   U   N  I  T  |  R  A  Y  E  |  N  E  M  E  A
   P   A  L  S  |  A  L  A  S  |  O  V  E  R [TURN]
```

68

```
B  O  Z  O  |  I  C  O  N  S  |  E  G  G [HEAD]
I  L  E  T  |  N  O  H  O  W  |  P  A  L  O
G  A  R  E  |  C  N  O  T  E  |  I  R  O  N
[HEAD] F  O  R  T  H  E  H  I  L  L  S  |
E  I  E  I  O  |  |  P  L  A  C  A  R  D
D  I  S  |  Y  U  A  N  | [HEAD] T  O  T  O  E
|  B  O  S  N  I  A  |  P  A  T  E
S  H  R  U  N  K  E  N  H  E  A  D  S
G  H  I  A  |  A  C  T  U  A  L  |
R  A  D  I  O [HEAD] |  E  S  T  S  |  S  O  B
E  W  E  N  E  C  K  |  E  A  T  M  E
|  D  R  A  W  B  R  I  D  G  E  A [HEAD]
A  N  T  E  |  S  I  R  E  N  |  L  E  H  I
X  E  N  A  |  E  K  I  N  G  |  E  L  A  N
[HEAD] E  N  D  |  S  E  G  U  E  |  T  E  N  G
```

69

```
T  M  A  N  |  E  M  I  L  |  O  H  J  O  Y
J  E  R  I  |  Y  O  D  A  |  B  U  E  N  O
M  A  R  M  |  E  B  A  Y  W  I  N  D  O  W
A  G  E  O  F  |  H  U  H  S  |
X  R  A  Y  O  F  H  O  P  E  |  L  I  V  E
X  E  R  |  C  I  A  |  E  V  O  K  E  D
|  T  U  R  B  A  N  L  E  G  E  N  D
C  B  E  R  S  |  L  I  E  |  T  O  A  D  Y
R  A  D  I  O  S  A  M  I  G  O  S  |
U  R  G  E  N  T  |  N  N  E  |  A  M  E
Z  E  E  S  |  A  W  E  S  C  R  A  V  E  N
|  D  R  A  X  |  S  Q  U  A  D
E  X  T  R  A  E  X  T  R  A  |  U  L  N  A
M  Y  B  A  D  |  E  O  N  S  |  A  S  I  S
O  Z  A  W  A  |  S  L  A  P  |  S  E  T  H
```

70

```
J  U  D  Y  |  C  L  A  D  |  N  O  V  A
O  P  I  E  |  R  U  B  E  |  A  B  E  L
A  T  T  S  |  M  I  N  I  M  O  Z  A  R  T
D  O  Z  I  N  G  B  A  T  |  R  A  M  B  O
|  D  U  M  |  N  O  R  A  S  |
C  A  R  O  M  |  S  E  R  E  N  E  |
U  T  E  |  B  O  O  Z  Y  W  O  N  D  E  R
J  O  N  I  |  S  N  I  D  E  |  E  A  V  E
O  Z  O  N  E  L  I  N  E  R  S  |  D  I  A
|  S  L  I  C  E  R  |  P  S  A  L  M
|  B  R  O  W  N  |  A  R  C  |
C  R  I  M  E  |  C  O  Z  Y  Y  O  U  N  G
L  I  O  N  S  D  O  Z  E  N  |  T  R  O  T
A  N  T  I  |  O  O  Z  E  |  I  S  S  O
M  E  S  A  |  S  P  Y  S  |  A  A  H  S
```

71

```
[HOOPY/CIRCLE] S  T  E  R  |  A  W  E  I  N  S  P  I [RING/ZERO]
   L  O  R  R  E  |  N  E  U  R  O  P  A  T  H
   I  M  A  M  S  |  T  A  L  K  R  A  D  I  O
   N  A  M  A  T  H  |  R  E  I  D  |  U  N  U
   E  S  S  |  A  D  A  R  N  |  M  A  A  R
   |  J  U  R  E  |  G  A  Y  |
   P  R  O  U  D  P  A  P  A  |  F  R  O  D  O
   R  O  U  N  D  S  T  H  E  C  O  R  N  E  R
   E  E  R  I  E  |  H  I  S  O  R  H  E  R  S
   |  O  R  I  |  O  D  E  S  |
   S  T  A  R  |  N  A  P  P  Y  |  A  N  C
   I  R  S  |  S  A  V  E  |  S  I  T  F  O  R
   Z  E  P  P  E  L  I  N  S  |  T  H  O  R  O
   E  V  I  C  T  I  O  N  S  |  C  R  U  M  P
[RING/ZERO] I  N  T  H  E  N  E  W  |  H  U  L  A [HOOPY/CIRCLE]
```

72

```
A  B  C  |  A  G  R  E  E  D  |  C  L  U  E
B  R  O  |  P  U  E  N  T  E  |  H  E  N  S
B  A  R  N  E  Y  F  I  E  F  |  A  R  C  S
A  N  N  E  |  S  S  A  |  R  E  S  O  L  E
|  B  O  W  |  C  O  A  L  M  I  E  N
T  O  R  N  O  U  T  |  N  Y  U  |
S  N  E  A  K  P  E  K  E  |  L  I  F  E  R
A  M  A  T  |  S  C  O  U  R  |  N  I  T  E
R  Y  D  E  R  |  H  A  P  P  Y  F  E  T  E
|  O  B  I  |  S  I  M  I  L  E  S
S  N  O  W  C  O  E  N  |  A  D  D  |
C  U  B  I  S  M  |  A  E  R  |  E  M  M  A
A  R  A  L  |  B  O  R  D  E  R  L  I  E  N
B  S  M  T  |  A  R  C  A  N  A  |  C  A  T
S  E  A  S  |  Y  E  S  M  E  N  |  E  L  S
```

73

R	E	A	D	S		C	A	Y	S		I	P	O	S
A	T	A	R	I		O	B	O	E		M	I	R	A
N	U	R	S	E	S	A	I	D	A		P	E	E	R
I	D	O		S	E	R	T	A		C	O	C	O	A
S	E	N	A	T	E	S		B	A	R	R			
		N	A	M	E	T	H	A	T	T	U	N	A	
H	A	L	O	S		I	O	N	S		S	I	S	
A	M	E	N		T	A	P	E	S		S	T	N	S
N	I	X		M	O	P	S		U	P	S	E	T	
D	E	L	I	V	E	R	Y	D	A	T	A			
	U	M	P	S			E	M	E	R	G	E	D	
P	A	T	H	S		S	A	L	O	N		O	B	I
E	C	H	O		R	U	B	I	K	S	C	U	B	A
T	H	O	M		O	R	E	S		I	D	L	E	R
E	Y	R	E		B	E	T	H		L	I	D	D	Y

74

A	T	P	L	A	Y		U	N	I		P	C	T	S
D	I	R	I	G	I	B	L	E	S		R	A	H	S
E	L	E	V	E	N	+	T	W	O		O	S	I	S
E	S	S	E	S		A	R	T	L	O	V	E	R	
P	I	T	T		O	V	A		D	R	I	F	T	S
	T	O	H	A	V	E		N	E	E	D	I	E	R
			M	E	R	L	E			E	L	E	A	
B	I	C		A	N	A	G	R	A	M		E	N	S
E	T	U	I		G	A	V	E	L					
L	A	T	T	I	C	E		O	R	I	N	G	S	
A	D	R	E	N	O		Q	U	O		O	R	C	S
	D	A	M	A	S	C	U	S		S	N	O	O	P
A	S	T	I		T	W	E	L	V	E	+	O	N	E
S	U	E	Z		A	T	E	Y	E	L	E	V	E	L
A	P	S	E		S	S	N		E	L	D	E	S	T

75

S	A	L		R	O	I	L			F	E	S	T	S
U	G	O		E	R	N	E		S	I	X	E	R	S
N	I	C	O	T	I	N	E		Y	A	P	P	E	R
S	T	A	N	D	B	Y		O	N	S	E	T	S	
E	A	T	S		I	C	O	N	O	C	L	A	S	T
T	T	O	P	S		R	E	P	O	S	T	E	D	
S	E	R	E	N	A		I	I	S		E	S	S	
		C	O	I	N	F	L	I	P	S				
D	B	L		R	O	I		S	T	O	L	A	F	
W	A	I	T	A	S	E	C		A	R	O	L	L	
I	N	C	O	M	P	L	E	T	E		T	I	T	O
	D	E	N	I	E	S		R	E	M	O	T	E	S
C	A	N	I	N	E		C	O	N	I	F	E	R	S
M	I	S	T	E	D		E	M	I	L		R	E	E
I	D	E	E	S		O	P	E	D		S	D	S	

The New York Times

Crossword Puzzles

The #1 Name in Crosswords

Available at your local bookstore or online at nytimes.com/nytstore

---

Recent Releases

Holiday Spirit Crosswords	978-1-250-07539-0
Large-Print Train Your Brain	
Crossword Puzzles	978-1-250-07545-1
Rainy Day Crosswords	978-1-250-07541-3
Sunday Crossword Puzzles, Volume 41	978-1-250-07544-4
Thrilling Thursday Crosswords	978-1-250-07543-7
Tons of Puns Crosswords	978-1-250-07540-6
Will Shortz's Favorite Puzzlemakers	978-1-250-03255-3
Wonderful Wednesday Crosswords	978-1-250-07542-0
Best of Friday Crosswords	978-1-250-05590-3
Best of Saturday Crosswords	978-1-250-05591-0
Easy as Pie Crosswords	978-1-250-05592-7
Piece of Cake Puzzles	978-1-250-05594-1
Coffee Shop Crosswords	978-1-250-06336-6
Cup of Tea and Crosswords	978-1-250-06333-5
Extra Easy Crosswords	978-1-250-06338-0
Marvelous Monday Crosswords	978-1-250-06339-7
Terrific Tuesday Crosswords	978-1-250-06340-3

Special Editions

'Tis the Season Crosswords	978-1-250-05589-7
Will Shortz Presents The Crossword Bible	978-1-250-06335-9
Winter Wonderland Crosswords	978-1-250-03919-4
Pocket-Size Puzzles: Crosswords	978-1-250-03915-6
Will Shortz Picks His Favorite Puzzles	978-0-312-64550-2
Crosswords for the Holidays	978-0-312-64544-1
Crossword Lovers Only: Easy Puzzles	978-0-312-54619-9
Crossword Lovers Only: Easy to	
Hard Puzzles	978-0-312-68139-5
Little Black & White Book of Holiday	
Crosswords	978-0-312-65424-5
Little Black (and White) Book of Sunday	
Crosswords	978-0-312-59003-1
Will Shortz's Wittiest, Wackiest	
Crosswords	978-0-312-59034-5
Crosswords to Keep Your Brain Young	978-0-312-37658-8
Little Black (and White) Book of	
Crosswords	978-0-312-36105-1
Will Shortz's Favorite Crossword Puzzles	978-0-312-30613-7
Will Shortz Presents Crosswords for	
365 Days	978-0-312-36121-1

Easy Crosswords

Easy Crossword Puzzles Volume 15	978-1-250-04486-0
Easy Crossword Puzzles Volume 16	978-1-250-06337-3
Volumes 2–14 also available	

Tough Crosswords

Tough Crossword Puzzles Vol. 13	978-0-312-34240-3
Tough Crossword Puzzles Vol. 12	978-0-312-32442-1
Volumes 9–11 also available	

Sunday Crosswords

Snowed-In Sunday Crosswords	978-1-250-05595-8
Sunday Crossword Puzzles Volume 40	978-1-250-05596-5
Smart Sunday Crosswords Volume 1	978-1-250-06341-0

Sweetheart Sunday Crosswords	978-1-250-06334-2
Sweet Sunday Crosswords	978-1-250-01592-6
Sunday Crossword Puzzles Volume 38	978-1-250-01544-0
Sunday in the Surf Crosswords	978-1-250-00924-1
Simply Sundays	978-1-250-00390-4
Fireside Sunday Crosswords	978-0-312-64546-5
Snuggle Up Sunday Crosswords	978-0-312-59057-4
Stay in Bed Sunday Crosswords	978-0-312-68144-9
Relaxing Sunday Crosswords	978-0-312-65429-0
Finally Sunday Crosswords	978-0-312-64113-9
Crosswords for a Lazy Sunday	978-0-312-60820-0
Sunday's Best	978-0-312-37637-5
Sunday at Home Crosswords	978-0-312-37834-3

Omnibus

More Monday Crossword Puzzles	
Omnibus Vol. 2	978-1-250-04493-8
More Tuesday Crossword Puzzles	
Omnibus Vol. 2	978-1-250-04494-5
Monday Crossword Puzzle Omnibus	978-1-250-02523-4
Tuesday Crossword Puzzle Omnibus	978-1-250-02526-5
Crossword Puzzle Omnibus Vol. 16	978-0-312-36104-1
Sunday Crossword Omnibus Vol. 10	978-0-312-59006-2
Easy Crossword Puzzles Omnibus	
Volume 10	978-1-250-04924-7
Previous volumes also available	

Portable Size Format

Will Shortz Presents A Year of Crosswords	978-1-250-04487-7
Curious Crosswords	978-1-250-04488-4
Bedside Crosswords	978-1-250-04490-7
Crosswords to Supercharge Your Brainpower	978-1-250-04491-4
Best of Sunday Crosswords	978-1-250-04492-1
Teatime Crosswords	978-1-250-04489-1
Soothing Sunday Crosswords	978-1-250-03917-0
Best of Wednesday Crosswords	978-1-250-03913-2
Best of Thursday Crosswords	978-1-250-03912-5
Sunday Crossword Puzzles Volume 39	978-1-250-03918-7
Will Shortz Wants You to Solve Crosswords!	978-1-250-04918-6
Crosswords to Start Your Day	978-1-250-04919-3
Crosswords For Your Commute	978-1-250-04923-0
Easy Does It Crosswords	978-1-250-04920-9
Relax and Unwind Crosswords	978-1-250-03254-6
Smart Sunday Crosswords	978-1-250-03253-9
Homestyle Crosswords	978-1-250-01543-3
Picnic Blanket Crosswords	978-1-250-00391-1
Huge Book of Easy Crosswords	978-1-250-00399-7
Keep Calm and Crossword On	978-0-312-68141-8
Best of Monday Crosswords	978-1-250-00926-5
Best of Tuesday Crosswords	978-1-250-00927-2
Mad About Crosswords	978-1-250-00923-4
All the Crosswords That Are Fit to Print	978-1-250-00925-8
For the Love of Crosswords	978-1-250-02522-7
Sweet and Simple Crosswords	978-1-250-02525-8
Surrender to Sunday Crosswords	978-1-250-02524-1
Easiest Crosswords	978-1-250-02519-7
Will's Best	978-1-250-02531-9
Other volumes also available	

St. Martin's Griffin

Printed in Great Britain
by Amazon

52015488R00056